THE WAY
I SEE IT

*A Psychologist's Guide to a
Happier Life*

BY DR. ASHLEY SMITH

Edited by Lil Barcaski

Published by: GWN Publishing
www.GWNPublishing.com

Cover Design: Kristina Conatser

ISBN: 978-1-959608-88-2

DEDICATION

To my dad, David, who has always been in my corner and has never failed to let me know he's proud. Thank you for always showing up, cheering me on, and encouraging me to chase bigger dreams than I could imagine. I love you, Pops.

TABLE OF CONTENTS

INTRODUCTION

Giving up my car keys was the hardest decision of my life. That moment marked a stark contrast between my Before and After.

THE BEFORE

In the Before, I was able to pass for "normal," hiding my vision impairment. I was able to fake sight well enough that most people, even those close to me, didn't realize the extent of my vision loss.

You see, I have a rare degenerative retinal disease called Occult Macular Dystrophy that makes me legally and increasingly blind. As a child, it was clear that I had inherited my grandmother's "bad eyes." Nothing was blurry. I just couldn't see some stuff, and the amount of stuff that I couldn't see expanded over time. I went from being able to read the chalkboard from the back of the classroom to struggling to read it from the front. There were no answers for why I couldn't see, and glasses helped only marginally.

Still, I was bright and capable, and I used those skills to my advantage. Relying on a combination of memory, context clues, and excuses, I was able to function really well without letting on that I have a blind spot in my central vision.

I made it through college with flying colors and went on to graduate school where I studied happiness and anxiety, earning my PhD in clinical psychology. Two years out of school, I landed my dream job. I had a thriving career doing something I enjoyed, good friends, and a little too much fun, all the while masking a part of who I really am.

As one of my closest friends, another psychologist who had the inside scoop about my eyes, told me once, "You're adhering to the faulty belief that you're flawed."

"I AM flawed," I told her.

I believed it. Wholeheartedly. My vision set me apart from others. If they knew, they'd reject me. Period. So I hid it.

Until the moment I couldn't hide it anymore.

THE AFTER

Faking sight is fine… until it comes to driving. When I knew I could no longer safely do it, I made the decision to give up my keys. It was terrifying because it meant explaining to people why I don't drive, which felt like putting a flashing neon sign over my head that said, "Flawed. Less than. Doomed."

In the After, I was devastated. My life as I knew it was over. There was no way I could be happy. I wouldn't be able to be successful or independent. I was convinced I wouldn't be loved or accepted. In the face of those supposed truths, I spent a lot of time wrapped up in grief and fear and sadness.

It turns out, though, that I was wrong. None of those "truths" panned out. It's been a journey of learning to accept things I cannot control and how to be happy despite them.

As they say, it is darkest before dawn. While life feels light and joyful now, I cannot honestly say that I would choose (legal) blindness. Still, I am grateful for the lessons I have learned and the ways in which my experiences, both professionally and personally, have shaped who I am and the way I approach life.

I am no longer sad or scared about my vision. It is simply something that I live with, and it's no longer even a defining feature of my day-to-day experience. In fact, it's really just an inconvenience at times and a non-issue at others. I feel like I have come a long way toward cracking the code of how to live a good life, regardless of the curveballs that get thrown at you. I am not immune to despair or doubt. I am not perfect. But I hope to look back on my life—ideally, decades from now—with gratitude to Past Ashley for what she's done and how she's lived.

THE INSIDE SCOOP

I have a unique skill set and body of knowledge, courtesy of my job as a clinical psychologist. I am fascinated by our brains and the way they process information. The glitchy things twist our perceptions and jump to conclusions, often distorting reality in ways that we don't even realize, at least not without a solid foundation in psychology and a lot of self-reflection.

My profession has served me well. I have had the luxury of being inundated with therapy through years of training and supervision followed by even more years of practicing with others, guiding their journeys of overcoming fear and insecurity. Many of my closest friends are also therapists, beautifully insightful, deep individuals who love me enough to call me on my bullshit and to have hard conversations when needed. I live and breathe psychology. I think about thinking every day. I consider the path toward happiness and how our actions and mindsets propel us forward or backward on that path.

I know that I would not be where I am or who I am without psychology, and I wish everyone knew what I do about our minds and how they work. There would be so much less suffering and so many more people living big, bold lives if they did.

My formal training and my desperate personal journey for happiness, the experiences I've had, the people who have influenced and guided me, have all coalesced into this place in which I am confident and content. I am excited by life and able to weather its storms with resilience, trust, and hope.

I want the same for you.

I hope that my mark on this world is that I inspire someone to think differently. That desire is what led me to co-found Peak Mind: The Center for Psychological Strength with my dear friend, Dr. April Seifert. We share a mission to help people like you and me build psychological strength so that we can thrive—not just survive— through life's ups and downs. For several years, I have written our blog posts and articles, which are part teaching core psychological concepts and part processing life lessons I've learned. This book is a collection of some of those pieces as well as other ideas that tie them together, all with the intention of helping you live a happier life.

This is the way I see it.

SECTION 1

The Mind Games We Play

I f there is one thing I wish everyone knew, it is this: You can't believe everything you think. Our minds are amazing... but they are the source of so much unnecessary suffering.

What we think has a huge impact on how we feel and what we do. Take, for example, this scenario. Your boss says, "We need to talk." If you, like so many others, automatically jump to *Oh no! What did I do? Am I going to get in trouble? Fired?!* then you'll feel anxious. On the other hand, if your first thought is *Awesome! I bet she wants to talk about that project I just nailed*, you'll go into that meeting feeling excited and confident. Same situation. Two very different reactions.

It's not just *what* we think but also *how* we think that matters. Like your favorite social media platform's algorithm that sorts through endless posts and videos to serve you up a curated feed, our minds do much the same thing. Outside of our conscious awareness, our minds sift through tons of information, taking shortcuts that lead to biased thinking. We move through our days without even realizing just how much of our experiences and our perspectives are being shaped by these behind-the-scenes processes.

When left to their own devices, our minds' natural tendencies skew negative. They look for problems, focus on what's wrong, ruminate, worry, expect the worst, criticize, and judge. While there's a time and place for all of this, our minds will run amok, to our detriment, if we let them.

The more you know about how your mind works… and how to make it work for you… the better. As we like to say at Peak Mind, your mind can be your most valuable asset or your biggest liability. You get to choose.

Make the right choice.

OUR TWO WORLDS

We all inhabit two worlds simultaneously. One is our shared world, the *External World*. The other is private to each of us, our *Internal World*. Most of the time, our worlds blend, somewhat seamlessly to us. That's both a good thing and a not so good thing.

Things can get messy when our worlds collide, especially when it's unanticipated or, worse, happening without our awareness. But let's back up a minute and look at these two worlds.

OUR EXTERNAL WORLD

When you think of the world you live in, the External World is likely what you're considering. When you open your eyes and look around at trees and buildings that everyone else can see, you're experiencing the External World. When you hear children laughing or birds chirping or horns honking, again, this is the External World. When hurricanes destroy homes, when laws are enforced, when the sun rises and sets… that's all the External World.

We know this world through our sensory experiences, the things we can see, hear, smell, taste, and touch. And while there may be differences in our perceptions, these are experiences we can share.

OUR INTERNAL WORLD

Truly knowable only to us, our Internal World consists of the things we experience within the confines of our skin. Everything we think. Everything we feel. Our memories, assumptions, expectations, interpretations. The meaning we ascribe to events. Our identity. Our beliefs.

Our Internal Worlds exist to help us understand and function in the External World. Our remembered histories and our imagined futures inform us, providing valuable insights we can use to navigate our shared world. Our thoughts and our feelings shape the way we operate, the choices we make, and the things we do and don't do.

But sometimes our intel, our Internal World, is skewed or distorted, maladaptive or otherwise unhelpful.

WORLDS SHAPING WORLDS

We learn about how the External World works based on what we observe. Events that happen to us and experiences that we go through stamp our memories, cultivate our beliefs, and craft our identities and world views. Thus, the External World helps to mold our Internal World.

In turn, beliefs—Internal World inhabitants—act as filters, skewing our vision of the External World. That skewed perception drives certain actions, which garner more experiences that confirm that very perception.

For example, the Internal World mandate that the world is a terrible place full of selfish people may lead us to engage in defensive actions, self-protective and self-serving behaviors, or low tolerance or patience for others. The result may be negative reactions from others, which we interpret as proof of that "fact." Meanwhile, someone who views the world as a great place full of caring awesome humans, again a perception, the purview of their Internal World, may enact an opposite self-fulfilling prophecy. Assuming generous motives from others and responding in kind, they create a different kind of External World experience.

WHEN WORLDS COLLIDE

Our Internal and External Worlds are intricately intertwined, informing and reacting to each other in a delicate, reciprocal dance. Sometimes, the wrong twist or turn results in a stutter step, which, over time, may have dire consequences.

Our thoughts and feelings are real, but they may not accurately reflect reality, another word for our shared experiences in the External World. They belong in our private, Internal Worlds. Yet, we project them outside all the time and treat them as capital-T-Truth.

And that's when problems arise.

Sometimes instead of providing helpful guidance on how to navigate or make sense of the External World, our Internal Worlds—our thoughts and feelings—dominate our field of vision, and we react to them IN THE EXTERNAL WORLD as though they are inevitable, unalterable, objective facets of reality.

Stay with me.

Conflict with your partner happens. But is it in the shared External World or are you fighting separate fights in your own Internal Worlds?

You expected (your Internal World) him to do the dishes. He did not (External World). You sarcastically comment about not being a maid (External). He rolls his eyes (External) because you always act like a martyr (his Internal World). You're hurt because he takes you for granted (your Internal). You feel unloved and unappreciated (your Internal). He feels dejected because no matter what he does, it's not enough (his Internal).

So many hurt feelings, so many thoughts—*martyr, not enough, unappreciated*. So many private experiences projected onto a sink full of dishes.

Other Internal World manifesting in the External World scenarios:

* Self-sabotaging a relationship (External) because you "know" it's not going to work (prediction = Internal World).

* Having an imaginary conversation with someone who has wronged you (Internal World) rather than directly confronting the situation and having a hard conversation (External World). Conversely, thinking about how much someone means to you but not saying it out loud, expecting that they'll just know.

* Accepting poor treatment from others (External) because you're not worthy (belief = Internal).

* Honking at the driver speeding past you (External) because they're a selfish jerk (interpretation = Internal).

* Feeling disappointed or angry (Internal) and acting accordingly (External) because your expectations weren't met (Internal).

* Missing out on what your child or boss told you (External) because you were daydreaming (Internal).

There are countless other times when we take our Internal World experiences—our thoughts, feelings, assumptions, meanings, memories, and expectations—as facts of the External World or assume that others will just know, completely agree with, or intuit our private, inside experiences.

Our Internal Worlds are powerful and useful and completely natural, and we're not going to escape them for any significant length of time. The goal, really, is to be aware that it exists and that it is separate from the External World. We must also hold onto the knowledge that as real as it is to us, it may not be real to others, and it certainly can't be known to them unless we do a heck of a good job communicating it to them.

Take charge of your Internal World. If it's a scary place, change it. Create an enriching Internal World, one in which you can thrive. Do some self-reflection. Pay attention to how it works, how it influences your actions in the External World, and whether your worlds are in harmony or not. If not, build your psychological strength and work to align the two.

"Your mind is an entire world..."

—MATSHONA DHLIWAYO

HOW YOUR MIND IS HOLDING YOU BACK

I love to think of our brains and minds as amazing and powerful biological computers. The interaction of the hardware (brain) and software (mind) not only keeps us alive, but it makes us who we are and drives us to do the things we do.

Just like our computers have operating systems and programs that run behind the scenes allowing them to interact with the outside world, so do we. From day 1, our minds are constantly scanning our environments, taking in information, and forming programs and rules about how the world works and our place in it. These programs—which are just deeply held beliefs—serve as the filters through which we see the world. They govern how we process our experiences, drive our reactions, and dictate our decisions and actions.

For example, if you have a program that says skills and abilities are things that can be learned and developed, you're likely to try new things, not get discouraged by failure, especially early on, and to persevere until you master it. In contrast, if your programming holds that skills and abilities are innate or natural, then you are likely to give up quickly if you are not immediately good at something, or you may not even try it because there's no point. (These specific programs, by the way, are called growth mindset and fixed mindset, respectively.)

Much of our programming is quite helpful or, perhaps, innocuous. Some of it, though, is quite problematic.

SELF-LIMITING BELIEFS

You may have heard the term "self-limiting beliefs" before. These are beliefs—subconscious programming or rules—that hold you back in some way. The rub is that it's the *beliefs* that are holding you back, not *reality*.

There's a classic story that really highlights the power of self-limiting beliefs. I first heard it on an episode of *Westworld* a few years ago, but it's all over the place. It goes something like this:

A traveler comes across a giant elephant being held in place by a rope tied to a tiny stake and asks the owner, "Why doesn't it just run away?"

The owner replies, "Because it doesn't know it can. You see, when it was just a baby, it was held in place by that same rope. At first, it struggled and pulled against the rope trying to get free. It was too small and weak though, so it gave up."

Of course, *we* know that a full-grown elephant is one of the largest and strongest animals out there, but it doesn't know its true power.

UNCOVERING YOUR SUBCONSCIOUS PROGRAMMING

Because so much of this operates behind the scenes in our brains, we're often not aware of the deep down belief systems that impact us.

As a psychologist, I think about thinking. Every. Single. Day. I like to think I'm pretty self-aware and have uncovered and revised a lot of my unhelpful, self-limiting beliefs, but there's always more work to be done.

As you know, I have a visual impairment that makes me legally blind. I've done a lot of work over the years to let go of self-limiting beliefs like *I am flawed. I am less than because of my vision.* I thought I had made a lot of progress in reprogramming my mind, but a real breakthrough happened a few years ago.

Every so often, my vision shifts for the worse. I get some telltale symptoms like wobbly focus and headaches for a few days, then it stops, and I've lost a bit more sight. These shifts happen unpredictably, and they used to really freak me out.

I was out for a run one night and the wobbling started, followed by me, of course, freaking out. I was scared and sad, but I couldn't talk to anyone about it because of the rejection that I thought would inevitably happen. I felt completely alone.

Except that I wasn't.

I had an Aha moment as I realized that it was the *belief* that no one will want me if they knew the extent of my flaw that was making me feel alone. This rope was holding me back from talking with my then-partner about what I was experiencing. That lightbulb was powerful. I picked up my phone and called. I told him what was going on and that I was scared... and he listened and supported me. And I felt so much better.

I still don't love when the wobbling starts, but I don't freak out much anymore. I've been able to break some of those ropes that were holding me back. I wonder, though, *what ropes are holding you back?*

CHANGING YOUR PROGRAMMING

By definition, subconscious processes happen outside of our conscious awareness, which means that we're not readily tuned into them. They happen behind the scenes in a place we're not privy to. Fortunately, with effort, there are some things we can do to become more aware of our programming, and awareness is the first step in being able to change it.

Self-reflection

Taking time to reflect on our experiences, to really pause and consider what happened (especially internally) and why, can help. This reflection may take the form of quiet introspection, journaling, self-monitoring or tracking your reactions (like what you thought and how you felt in various situations), processing with a trusted person, or therapy. Regardless of how you do it, it's valuable.

Drilling Down

It's often easier to catch the surface-level automatic thoughts that run through our minds in any given situation. If you can grab one, you can drill down into it to uncover the deeper belief. Ask a series of questions like *If that is true, what would be so bad about that or what would it mean about me?* Continue drilling down until you get to the bottom.

For example, maybe you're stressed out because you're juggling kids, a project at work, and the usual household management tasks. You think *I'll never get it all done.* Then you drill down by asking yourself, "What would be bad and/or what would it mean about you if you don't get it all done?" Maybe it goes something like this:

- So, what would be so bad about not getting it all done? *I'll drop the ball at work and miss out on that promotion, and my kids will be impacted because I'm not spending quality time with them.*

- If that's true, what does it mean about you? *It means that I'm doing a bad job all around.*

- If that's true, what's so bad about that or what does that mean about you? *It means I'm a failure.*

- If that's true, what's so bad about that or what does that mean about you? *It means that I'm a terrible parent. I'm incapable.*

That right there is some deep dark programming that might be holding you back in some areas of life. What might you do to start changing it?

We don't get to choose our initial programming. It's like our minds download a bunch of apps before we're even able to consider whether we want them or need them. As we age, though, and gain agency, we can change that. While the original programming may always be there, we can cover it up with new, more helpful beliefs. Choose to do the work and break free from those mental ropes that are holding you back.

"The right belief is like a good cloak, I think. If it fits you well, it keeps you warm and safe. Wrong fit, however, can suffocate."

—WIT in *The Final Empire* by Brandon Sanderson

TENDING YOUR MIND'S GARDEN: CULTIVATING THE RIGHT BELIEFS

I like metaphors. They make complex concepts easy to understand and have a way of just making things click. One I'm chewing on is that your mind is a garden with thoughts and beliefs being the plants that grow there. That concept leads to questions like: What gets planted and by whom? What flourishes and what gets weeded out? In other words, how do you tend your mental garden?

WHAT GETS PLANTED AND WHY: HOW BELIEFS ARE FORMED

Some people love the Southwestern part of the U.S., with its red rocks, deserts, and the cacti and other native vegetation that thrive in that dry climate. I can appreciate the beauty there, but I'm drawn to the tropics, plants with rich green shiny leaves and vibrant flowers, the ones that do best with lots of sun and lots of rain. One isn't inherently better than the other, but they are undeniably different.

We are all born into certain cultures and contexts. Think of it like being born in New Mexico v. Hawaii. The native plants are quite different. They belong there naturally and are going to easily take root and grow in your garden. In fact, you may not even really have to create a garden. Without any effort on your part, those plants will be there.

Such is the case with our minds. Many of our deeply rooted beliefs are native plants. They're there naturally as a function of where we are born and raised. We don't even question it. Of course, there are cacti in the desert and lush green leaves in the rainforest. That's just how it is. Many of our foundational beliefs, the rules that guide us through the world, were native plants. They weren't planted by us or with our consent or even awareness.

So Where Do Beliefs Come From?

From day 1, our minds are busy processing all of the information coming in through our five senses. They look for patterns so they can develop shortcuts, which save energy, speed up processing, and, ultimately, help our minds do their number one job of keeping us alive.

Beliefs are things that our minds take to be facts. These are the conclusions they've drawn about what things mean, how to stay safe in a variety of contexts, how the world works, and our place in it. Beliefs are the lessons our minds learn, and there are two ways that this learning occurs.

Explicit Learning

Explicit learning is probably what you think of when you think about learning. This is intentional learning. When you sat down as a student to study history facts or learn science concepts, you were engaging in explicit learning.

Some of our beliefs are planted in this way. We are directly told that there is or isn't a God, that climate change is or isn't real, that people like us hold the door open for others, that big girls and boys don't cry, that exercise is good for you, that touching toilets is yucky, whatever. Other people directly instruct us. We read books, have conversations, watch videos, listen to lectures, mull over the information, and intentionally accept it or reject it. We plant beliefs in our garden, at least once we're old enough and our brains are formed enough to do that. Prior to that point, someone else does the planting, while we watch and trust that this is what is supposed to be in our garden.

Implicit Learning

This is a sneakier kind of learning. It happens behind the scenes, out of your awareness, in your subconscious. Whether you realize it or not, your mind is constantly learning and creating beliefs based on your experiences.

For example, as an American woman born in the 80s, I was raised on television, magazines, and Barbie dolls that featured a certain beauty ideal—tanned white skin, blonde hair, thin waist, ample bosom. That image, combined with the myriad advertisements about weight loss supplements and programs, beauty enhancement products, and makeup as well as whatever personal experiences I've had, gave my mind a clear message that there is one way to be beautiful and that most natural bodies aren't it. For women like me, our minds concluded that we are not enough in the looks department. Is it any wonder that the majority of American (and places that have American media) women do not feel good about their bodies? It's less to do with our actual bodies and more to do with what got planted in our mind's garden.

Beliefs related to body image are an easy one to highlight, as is race, gender, religion, and political standpoints. But we've got native plants, implicitly learned, about literally everything. About emotions—which ones are good and bad, which ones are okay to express, and how we are supposed to feel; people—setting boundaries or not, being vulnerable or not, how to connect or handle conflict; whether the world is safe or not; our abilities and worthiness. Every. Damn. Thing.

Every experience, particularly ones that are repeated or are very impactful (i.e., highly emotional), teaches our mind something. We're just not always aware of what's getting planted or being discriminating about whether we even want it in our garden or not.

TENDING THE GARDEN: HOW TO CHANGE YOUR BELIEFS

We do not have to be passive bystanders when it comes to our mind gardens. With the right knowledge and tools, we can actively shape and cultivate our belief systems.

Identifying Beliefs

A friend stopped by one day to get some cuttings from one of my house plants. "Is this a [insert some plant name I've never heard before]?"

"I have no idea," I replied. It wasn't a plant I had picked out or purchased, and I really didn't know what it was.

Most people are running around in much the same way, with no idea about the plants that are in their mental gardens. It takes a bit of self-reflection and introspection to really identify what's deeply rooted in our subconscious, to spell out the contents of our belief systems, especially with regard to those beliefs that were formed implicitly. That's the first step when it comes to designing and creating the belief system that truly works for you. Once we recognize what plants are in our gardens, that is, what we truly believe, especially deep down on the core belief level (these are our foundational beliefs and rules that act as the lenses through which we view the world), we can start to make some changes. We can decide if each plant is one we want to keep. If so, we cultivate it, tend to it, nourish it, and let it grow. If not, we weed it out.

Creating New Beliefs

With plants, "tending" means giving it the right amount of sunlight and water and clearing away weeds that might strangle it. When it comes to beliefs, this tending comes in the form of giving it attention. The more we focus on a thought and the more credibility we give it, the more we will have it. But even more so, we cultivate a belief through our behavior. We must act as though that belief is a fact that we are 100% certain about.

If we're dealing with a delicate seedling that we've just intentionally planted—for example, that my body is beautiful as is and deserves to be cared for—then we have to intentionally act on that belief. To do that, I might stop complaining about feeling fat, say "thank you" rather than making a self-disparaging or dismissive comment when someone gives me a compliment, or wear something that feels like it draws attention to the parts of my body I feel self-conscious about. It might mean making a point to intentionally focus on the parts of my appearance that I like when I look in a mirror rather than the barrage of negativity that comes for many people. All these actions will help this new belief take root, grow, and blossom.

WEEDING THE GARDEN: ELIMINATING UNHELPFUL BELIEFS

In contrast, when you identify a belief that does not serve you, that you want to pluck from your garden, you must either cut it down or let it wither away.

Cutting down a belief is something that psychologists call thought challenging. You'll also hear it called logical or rational thinking or, if we're being really technical, cognitive restructuring. This process involves taking a critical look at the evidence that supports the belief (you'll likely have a ready supply here) AND the evidence that refutes or challenges the belief. This part is a little harder. But if you really try, you're likely to find evidence or reasons not to buy into that belief anymore. You can draw alternative conclusions, then tend those new beliefs until they take root and become strong on their own.

You can also let mental weeds wither away by not tending them. It's the equivalent of keeping a plant in the dark with no water. It'll eventually shrivel up and die. With beliefs, we have to stop giving them attention. First, recognize it for what it is: a belief, a mental weed. It is not an absolute fact or an unalterable aspect of reality. Then, simply label it—*There's that old belief* or *There's that worry*—then pay attention to something else. Let the mental weed starve for attention.

You really speed up the withering process when you no longer let that belief dictate your actions or the choices you make. It's the exact opposite of cultivating a new belief. When we're trying to wither a weed, you have to stop letting it boss you around. You have to break that mental rule. If I believe deep down that others will judge the real me if they get to know me AND I don't want that in my garden anymore, then I have to stop acting on it. That means stop hiding or masking, stop trying to control what others think of me. I have to be brave enough to show the real me and see what happens. By not letting that old belief dictate my actions anymore, it will start to wither away.

SORTING WEEDS FROM DESIRED PLANTS: WHICH BELIEFS ARE RIGHT?

While some people find gardening and yardwork enjoyable, I decidedly find it to be a chore. Having an enviable yard with pristine landscaping is so low on my list of priorities that I do the bare minimum. That meant that I let some weeds grow, completely unchecked. These guys are now several feet tall... and starting to bloom with flowers! I was talking to a friend about it, and they made a comment to the effect of "Well, who decides if it's a weed or not anyways?"

I guess I do. If I like it, if I find beauty in it, why can't I let it be in my flower bed? Who says my beds have to conform to whatever was here before or whatever people around me say?

The same is true for our beliefs. You may find as you intentionally cultivate your mind's garden that some things you were taught were natural or beautiful or necessary are actually not a requirement. You can get rid of those. And, you can tend to and grow some things that others might call weeds.

It's up to each of us to not only become aware of the intricacies of our belief systems, which will give us a deeper understanding of how we tick and why we do the things we do, but it is on each of us to take responsibility for becoming the master gardener by intentionally and thoughtfully shaping our mental landscape so that we can live the lives we want.

"Your mind is the garden, your thoughts are the seeds, the harvest can either be flowers or weeds."

—WILLIAM WORDSWORTH

THERE IS NO DELETE BUTTON IN YOUR BRAIN

Have you ever wanted to get rid of a thought? Forget something that happened? Erase a memory? Unknow something? I'm guessing you've been frustrated by the fact that you can't.

I'm also guessing, simply based on the fact that you're human, that you've forgotten something important at some point or feel like you've lost skills or knowledge that you once had. That's also frustrating, but in a completely different way.

The bad news—and the good news—is that there is no delete button in our brains. We cannot selectively erase or remove unwanted content from our minds. Nor is anything in there ever really lost.

THE ALMA MATER POSSESSION

I loved the movie *Beetlejuice* as a kid. My favorite part was the scene in which Adam and Barbara, recently deceased ghosts, try to scare the new owners of their home into leaving by possessing them. The surprised owners and their dinner guests have their bodies overtaken as they involuntarily lip sync and dance to "Day-O."

I recently had the real-life equivalent happen.

I went to my nephew's graduation from the same high school I attended 25 years ago. I left my hometown in 1998 and rarely go back. I don't really keep in touch with anyone from my high school days and, honestly, I don't think about that phase of life very often. It's not like I block it out intentionally. It just seems like a lifetime ago.

While this proud aunt would've gone anywhere to watch R get his diploma, I was also really curious to see what it would feel like to be back in Texarkana. My last visit was more than a decade ago. Would it feel nostalgic? What memories would be unearthed?

Turns out... not a lot. I didn't feel a sense of connection—it hasn't been home in a long time—and I wasn't flooded with memories. Of course, the football stadium where the ceremony was held was familiar. I spent a lot of time there as a teenager; football in the South is a real thing. But that was about it.

Until the announcer instructed everyone to stand for the singing of the alma mater.

Did we even have an alma mater? I wondered as I stood up. I recalled my class yell, and no one forgets how to call the Hogs (*Woo, Pig Sooie!*), but I was drawing a huge blank on an official school alma mater.

Even as the music began, I was pretty convinced we didn't have one.

Then the crowd started singing.

AND SO DID I.

The long-buried words tumbled out of my mouth. I was surprised, to say the least.

My mouth continued to sing while my mind questioned. *What is happening? What's the next line? How do you even know these lyrics?* Until the words came out, I didn't even know what they were going to be. It was kind of surreal.

And solidified that there is no delete button in our brains.

BURIED BUT NOT LOST

Prior to that day, if you had told me I used to know my high school alma mater, I would've told you I had forgotten it. Same thing with most of calculus, French vocabulary, and other bits of knowledge and skills that I haven't accessed in years.

But we don't really forget, do we?

Psychological research has shown that even when we "forget" skills or knowledge, we relearn them much faster the second time around, demonstrating that it wasn't really ever completely gone.

Our experiences, what we've learned consciously and subconsciously, what we've been through... it's all in there somewhere. That old programming really never goes away. New programming may get laid down on top of it, but the old stuff is still there, buried somewhere in the recesses of our minds.

It's like covering up original hardwoods with linoleum and then carpet. You may just be aware of the carpet under your feet, but those other layers of flooring are there... and you can get to them if you dig.

This can be great news if you want to relearn things that seem lost. Know that it won't take as much time or effort to get it back, so jump right on in.

Understanding the levels of programming—the layers of flooring—can be helpful, too, if you're ever found yourself stumped trying to figure out why you do the things you do or react in the ways you tend to. There's old learning deep inside there that's getting activated.

The bad news is that you can't delete the things you want to.

THE MISSING DELETE BUTTON WORK AROUND

As much as I wish we could control-alt-delete and reboot our brains... without certain thoughts, feelings, or memories, it just doesn't work that way. Once you've had a thought, you're more likely to have it again, especially if that thought gets a reaction from you.

Our minds are a lot like toddlers sometimes. What happens when you hear a little cutie unknowingly blurt out a cuss word? If you laugh, they put that word on repeat, right? And if you get mad and tell them to stop? Same thing. Because toddlers love attention. If a behavior gets any sort of reaction from the surrounding grownups, the ~~tiny terrorist~~ toddler will persist.

And so do our minds.

If our minds throw a thought out at us and we react to it with, say, shock, horror, fear, or disgust. You guessed it. That thought is likely to keep popping up.

Life would be easier if we could delete that inside "ick" that doesn't serve us, but we can't. Instead, we have to essentially do the mental equivalent of time out. Simply ignore it until it fades.

And I don't mean ignore it in the way a lot of people put ignoring into practice, with huffs and puffs, scowls, and glares. That's actually all attention. Truly ignoring is acting as though it's not even happening and being completely unaffected by it.

When an unwanted thought shows up, simply acknowledge it as a thought—not a hateful, terrifying, disturbing, or bad thought, just a thought. Then tune it out as you go on about your business. Same thing with memories or feelings. Acknowledge them, then ignore while you go on about your business.

It's like saying, "No, thank you," to the toddler, letting them tantrum it out on the floor, while you Go. On. About. Your. Business.

It's not a fast process, but it's the best we've got when it comes to covering that grimy linoleum with more pleasing tile.

"You think you want to know something, and then once you do, all you can think about is erasing it from your mind."

—SUE MONK KIDD

MENTAL TIME TRAVEL

T ime travel has been a focus of science fiction and physics for decades. It's captured our imaginations with movies like *Back to the Future* and *Interstellar*. It has boggled our minds with unanswerable questions: What would happen if I met my Past Self? How much would it change things if I went back and squashed a bug in 1953? Personally, I like to think about time travel—the logistics of it, whether I'd choose to go to the past or the future and how far into each, what I would change if I could, what stocks I would buy before returning to Now. How amazing and helpful and terrifying would it be to have a time machine?

In a sense, we already do! Our minds are like our own personal flux capacitors that allow us to mental time travel every day.

MENTAL TIME TRAVEL

Because of some very cool mental features and abilities, the human brain has the capacity to create memories and relive the past as well as to envision the future. We can instantaneously be transported back or forward in time, sometimes without even realizing what's happening.

If you're anything like the average person, then you mental time travel about half of your waking day. *Nearly half the time*, we are mentally somewhere else besides the present moment. We visit the past or imagine the future. While there are beneficial reasons for these psychological trips, there are downsides, too.

Revisiting the Past

Our memories are pretty spectacular things, like storage cabinets holding all of our experiences and the lessons we've learned along the way. Trips down memory lane can serve a lot of purposes: to entertain and connect as we share our stories with others, to help us know who we are, to keep us from repeating painful mistakes, to allow us to heal from difficult experiences, and to help us alter our present emotional state. (Ever noticed that memories can bring up feelings?)

Contrary to what a lot of people believe, though, our memories are not like video recordings of events. They are not necessarily accurate, factual representations of what transpired. They're more like a Word document that we open—and edit—before saving it again. This is an important and deceptive feature with big implications.

Being able to rewrite our memories in a sense allows us to mental time travel and alter the course of our personal history. We can open up and revise a memory, leaving out details to make the story more humorous or sympathy-inducing. We can add silver linings that help us tweak the lessons we learned. We can put a new spin on that terrible experience so that we walk away feeling stronger and more capable or to preserve our integrity and absolve us of blame.

What's more is that we can make these alterations without even realizing that we're doing it, meaning that we can unknowingly alter the past and proceed in the present on this new timeline.

Fortunately, we can also be strategic with our revisionary history efforts. We can go back in time and change events (or at least their impact). While it may feel deliberate and inaccurate at first, over time, the new memory becomes fact to us.

Because of the way memory works, we can't necessarily trust our recollection of the past. This is especially important to keep in mind when mental time travel gets you stuck ruminating and regretting. It is quite possible that your mental time travel has altered the past so that your memories are skewed and things were not as bad as they seem.

Imagining the Future

Being able to revisit the past in our minds is helpful because it allows us to use the wisdom and lessons from our past experiences in the present. It also becomes the foundation for daydreaming about the future. When we mental time travel to the future, we imagine events that have not occurred yet, and we anticipate how our Future Selves will feel.

Visiting the future can be a wonderfully helpful tool. It allows us to envision the possible outcomes of various choices, to set goals and aspirations, and to act accordingly in the here and now, altering the trajectory of our lives.

On a less grand scale, mental time travel forward can keep us safe. We can fast forward 15 seconds and see the possibility of being hit by a car when crossing the street, so we alter the timeline by pausing to look both ways. Visiting our Elderly Selves in a vivid way, scoping out what our lives are like decades in the future, can provide motivation to contribute to retirement accounts or eat our vegetables. Our Present Selves construct a better future.

The downside of mental time travel to the future is that we can become bound by these visions. We visit a future in which we are really happy or really sad and make decisions accordingly... only to find out that vision was skewed. The joy we imagine feeling when we make a big purchase is tarnished in reality because it is tempered by heavy work stress. Or the heartbreak we anticipate when ending a relationship is softened because our psychological immune system kicks in or because other areas of life are going really well. We may also be bound by the future when we accept it as unalterable, inevitable and resign ourselves to stop trying or striving for what we want.

THE COST OF MENTAL TIME TRAVEL

We can't be in two places at once. While my body may be rooted firmly in the present, I—the core essence of my self—am not when I mentally time travel. As adaptive as it can be to go back in time or jump to the future in our minds, it comes with a cost: the present. It means that we miss out on the here and now, on what is unfolding in real time. And, if we are mentally time traveling nearly half of the time, we're missing out on a substantial portion of life. It's like squandering your most precious, non-renewable resource: time.

Mental time travel can also negatively impact the present, shading it with unnecessary pain and distress. Anxiety doesn't live in the here and now. It lives in the future. Maybe it's in the next five seconds or five minutes or five months or 50 years, but it is not about what is happening right here, right now. Depression doesn't live right here, right now, either. It often lives in the past (potentially a distorted, revisionist version of it) or perhaps in a bleak, hopeless version of the future. So much of our suffering arises from mental time travel rather than from our actual present experience.

HOW TO STOP MENTAL TIME TRAVELING

Even after considering some of its costs, I wouldn't want to stop mental time traveling altogether. If it weren't for being able to imagine my future happiness, I wouldn't have gone to grad school, and I certainly wouldn't have done some early morning fitness class called Core Worx. Those efforts were all based on being able to picture what life would be like with and without a career or good health. That said, it's important to be intentional about mental time travel and to be present more often, especially when not being present doesn't serve us.

Work on simply noticing when you are lost in thought, mentally time traveling. Then choose to bring your focus back to the present. This is called mindfulness, and it is the key to being present for more of your life. Practicing mindfulness helps you build the self-awareness necessary to even recognize when you are not present, and it gives you the attentional control required to come back to the present. It's not an easy thing, but with practice, you can be here. Now.

"Your future is whatever you make it, so make it a good one."

—MICHAEL J. FOX **as Marty McFly in** *Back to the Future*

WHEN IS WORRY HELPFUL?

"Don't worry. Be happy!"

Ah, those illustrious words of Bobby McPherrin. (It's a classic 80s song, in case I'm dating myself here.)

"In your life, expect some trouble. but when you worry you make it double."

Wise words set to a catchy tune.

JUST DON'T WORRY

I'd argue (and often do) that worry is a bad mental habit. And like most bad habits, they can be broken... if you are so inclined, though it's not quite as simple as *just don't do it*. If it were, no one would worry excessively.

And yet, there is a kernel of truth to the sentiment of just don't worry. While you can't really flip a switch in your brain to turn worry off, you can actually choose whether you want to indulge in that mental process or not.

That's where a lot of people get stuck.

WHY WE WORRY

Let's backtrack a bit to fully understand and appreciate the complexity of worry and why it's hard not to do it.

The Evolution of Worry

Our minds evolved essentially to keep us alive, and worry is a part of that process. Worry is the mental anticipation of things that could go wrong. It's identifying potential problems or bad things that could harm us in some way.

You can see how having this capability could be quite helpful. If our ancestors could anticipate (aka, worry) that a predator might be lurking in the brush, then they could avoid getting eaten. It was advantageous to expect bad things, as opposed to positive outcomes or events, because doing so allowed our ancestors to sidestep danger, living on to pass along their genes.

Thus, we are the descendants of worriers.

And now our minds have gone a bit rogue, worrying about things well beyond predators and physical safety. They worry about all kinds of other possibilities that could be bad in some way (though they often miscategorize what is truly bad and good. How many initially "bad" things ended up being blessings in disguise?)

You might point out that our mind's ability to predict bad things could be helpful because if we can anticipate problems, we can prevent them.

Perhaps.

But that line of thinking is what gets people stuck in worry.

Where Does Worry Lead?

Let's dive deeper into it. What often follows worry—the ever so intriguing *What if...*—is either spiraling or planning, the first of which is absolutely not helpful... ever. The latter is potentially helpful, but we'll come back to that.

Spiraling happens when we hop on the Worry Train and follow it all the way down the tracks. It starts with a little *What if...*, then snowballs into catastrophizing. All of sudden our minds jump from Point A to Point Z... and we're listening to it like it's an inevitability or a capital-T-Truth.

It's not.

So much of what we worry about never comes to pass... and not because our actions directly prevent it but because it was just a hypothetical that did not come to fruition. Besides, when has spiraling EVER led to something positive or helpful? No one feels better while spiraling. It wastes time and energy. And it doesn't lead to anything productive. Planning, on the other hand, can *sometimes* be helpful.

Let's return to that belief—*If I can anticipate a problem, then I can prevent it.* If that is, in fact, true, it stands to reason that planning is a helpful action to take.

Sometimes it is.

But sometimes all of that planning is actually just an attempt to feel more in control. It gives us something to do to help us feel like we have the power to affect change, to prevent heartache and strife, but do we? Or is it just a way of trying to feel more secure, safe, and less anxious or stressed in the face of uncertainty?

I mean, when has anything ever gone exactly according to plan? And how much time and mental energy have you dedicated to creating plans that you never even needed?

I bet your own experiences demonstrate, as mine certainly do, that you cannot anticipate and plan for every potentiality. Or, perhaps you can anticipate some things, but they are out of your control to stop or change. Again, worry-fueled planning gives you something to do, but it's ineffective.

WHEN IS WORRY HELPFUL?

Anticipating problems and coming up with a game plan can be helpful at times, but only under specific circumstances. It becomes really important to differentiate between what I call productive and unproductive worry. Productive worry may be worth your time and energy, while unproductive worry, you guessed it, is not.

Productive Worry

Productive worry focuses on three things:

1. Actual problems, as opposed to hypothetical ones

2. Things that are relevant right now, as opposed to at some distant point in the future

3. Things that you can control, as opposed to ones that you have no say in

If it's not a real problem, for today, that you can control, it's probably unproductive worry.

Unproductive Worry

Many people who seek out therapy for worry (and probably lots of "worrywarts" who struggle on their own) recognize that excessive worry is a problem. It makes them feel anxious, tense, unsettled. They want to stop. Yet they struggle to do so. Why?

It's because, deep down, there is a belief that worry is helpful. Expanding on that are adjacent beliefs like: *If I worry enough, I will be able to prevent the bad things from happening. If I don't worry, and something happens, it will be my fault. If I don't worry, I am being irresponsible.*

Lies, I tell you! Here's why. All those concepts overestimate two things:

1. **THE ACCURACY OF OUR PREDICTION CAPABILITIES.** Don't trust me on this one? Consider this. How many times have you heard the word "unprecedented" in the last few years? There are nearly eight billion people on the planet, all with brains designed to anticipate problems, and yet how many "unprecedented" events have we been through?

2. **OUR ABILITY TO CONTROL THINGS.** While we may *want* to control or dictate how things will unfold, so much of what we focus on via worry and planning is actually outside of our circle of control. All the variables that contribute to how things unfold are simply not up to us. You can lament that they *should* be, but denying reality as it is isn't any more helpful than unproductive worrying.

FINE. THEN HOW DO I STOP WORRYING?

I wish it were as easy as just don't do it, flip the worry switch to off, and go on your merry way. The reality, though, is that it takes work.

First, recognize the mental process of worry. If it starts with a *What if*, it's a worry. Period. Even if it's *But what if this isn't a worry?*

What if = worry.

Other signals might be the *Oh nos*, or the sneakier predictions, the mental statements made with certainty—*This is going to happen. Then, this is going to happen.* That's still worry if you are anticipating future negative events. And as convincing as those thoughts might sound, they are predictions, not facts. No one has a crystal ball.

Once you recognize the mental process as worry, call it that. Then, choose what to do.

If it's a productive worry—an actual problem, for today, that you can control—then decide when you are going to do some strategic thinking, planning, and problem solving.

Notice that word "strategic." That means you are intentionally sitting down to tackle the issue. This is a very different experience than distractedly worrying and halfway coming up with a plan while also having a conversation with someone or watching your kid's soccer game. Strategic thinking—productive worry—happens intentionally on your timetable and has a designated end: a solution.

If you find yourself circling over the same territory repeatedly, rehashing plans, then you have ventured into unproductive worry.

More time will not get you more control, more certainty, more peace, or more guarantee of how the future will go.

At this point, you must directly challenge those metacognitions—those beliefs about worry. Get real with yourself. Is worrying about this *actually* going to make a difference? Does it just *feel* more comfortable to worry because that's what you've always done or because that's what your mind wants to do?

Choose to disengage from the mental process of worry and, instead, focus on something else, preferably the present moment. Come back to what's real right now and ask yourself, "How would I rather spend my precious time? Worrying or doing XYZ?"

"Don't worry. Be happy."

—BOBBY MCFERRIN

REDEFINING BAD: HOW CHANGING YOUR MINDSET CAN TRANSFORM YOUR LIFE

I feel a soapbox coming on. I hope you'll bear with me because the lesson here has the potential to make a real and noticeable impact on your life experience.

While I have spent some time diving into studies examining the neural circuitry of the amygdala, chemical switches in the brain, and how cognitive appraisal (i.e., how we think about a situation) impacts emotions on a brain level, I'll spare you the details.

What you need to know, in a nutshell, is that how we think about things affects how we feel and, ultimately, what we do. That's why it's so important to get a handle on how and what you think. And that's why I want to dig into the concept of "bad" and how over-played and unhelpful it really is.

WHAT IS BAD?

I love our brains. Those three pound (or 1,360 grams for every-one else who uses the much more logical metric system) biological computing powerhouses shape our entire life experience.

I am routinely awed and amused by them. Awed because of the sheer amount of information processing they are capable of and the complexity in their design. Amused because they are all kinds of glitchy.

If you're familiar with me, then you know I like to pull back the curtain on how our minds work, revealing the biases and distortions that are rampant in our thinking. Suffice it to say that our brains have developed shortcuts to help them do their jobs more efficiently. One of those shortcuts is judgments.

Our minds categorize things in an effort to be faster at processing information and directing us on how to respond. The simplest way to categorize is denoting something as "good" or "bad."

There is a rustling sound in the forest. A bear begins to emerge. It is large—many times bigger than I am. It has sharp teeth and long claws. It's moving quickly. Its hairs are standing up. That means it's not calm and friendly. It's growling. Oh no. It looks angry... or hungry. Bears can eat people. I'm people. Oh, no! I am in mortal danger! What do I do? I should run. No, that one article on Google said to make yourself bigger and louder to scare it away. I'm so scared! I don't want to die!

OR

Bear = Bad! Initiate survival sequence.

See how efficient it is for our brains to bypass all of the processing and thinking and jump straight to bad? And when our brains code something as bad, we automatically react to it in a base survival way—fight, flight, freeze, which translates to feeling anxious or angry and a strong desire to avoid or escape.

That works fine when we're dealing with bears, but what happens when other things get coded as bad?

FEELINGS AREN'T BAD

And here's the soapbox... How often do you say, "I feel bad"? If your answer is more than zero, buckle up. Bad is not a feeling. It's a judgment, a shortcut categorization that, as we've already established, initiates the avoid or escape sequence.

When we experience a natural feeling, albeit perhaps an unpleasant or difficult one like anxiety or sadness, and then code it as bad, what happens? Emotionally, we pile on more "ick." All of a sudden, we have extra anxiety or anger or guilt or shame on top of the original feeling.

It plays out like this: *I feel sad. Sad is BAD. Men shouldn't feel sad* (insert eye roll at horrifically unhelpful societal messaging). *Now I'm angry!*

Or this one: *I'm angry at my kids! What kind of mom gets angry over something like that? That's BAD. I shouldn't feel that way. Enter in guilt and sadness.*

When we label our feelings as bad, we're going to amplify our internal distress—pile on—or do things to avoid or escape feeling them. This point alone is worth the price of admission from a mental health and wellbeing standpoint, but let's dive into some more nuanced issues with our bad shortcut coding.

DIFFICULT IS NOT BAD

Our minds often default to difficult = bad. In part, it's because they were designed to keep us alive while expending the least amount of energy possible. Difficult takes energy, therefore it's bad.

But is it?

When middle school kids are taught that their struggle to learn new math concepts is actually a sign that their brains are making new connections and getting smarter (which it is, by the way), they persist. Their math scores go up, as does their confidence and cognitive computing power.

They embody a growth mindset, which encompasses the belief that difficult is not bad. It is necessary for growth and mastery.

Helpful.

DIFFERENT IS NOT BAD

We often feel uncomfortable, insecure, or anxious when we realize that what we want or how we are is different from others. Think about your own journey of self-acceptance. Maybe you're one of the lucky ones who was always comfortable marching to the beat of your own drum, but the rest of us have had to work, whether we realized it or not, on breaking the association of being different = being bad.

Different is just different. It's not better or worse until we add a value judgment to it.

We'd do well to remember that when it comes to other people, too, especially as the world gets smaller and we are continually encountering people with different belief systems. If we can just remember that different does not mean bad, we might be more open to being curious and compassionate, cutting down on unnecessary hostility and miscommunication.

DISCOMFORT IS NOT BAD

And my personal favorite: discomfort is not bad. It's simply uncomfortable or unpleasant, and there just might be a lot of value in being temporarily uncomfortable.

Growth of any kind requires discomfort.

Anxiety is uncomfortable (not bad), but the only way to overcome fear is to face it—to get comfortable being uncomfortable.

Learning a new skill can be uncomfortable—it can move you into unfamiliar territory where you don't feel competent—but how can you grow if you're not willing to be uncomfortable?

Change is uncomfortable, but does that mean bad? It's inevitable, so I certainly hope not. Take, for example, the discomfort that comes along with starting a new job, at least until we get up to speed and adjust to the new role. How many of us are still working at our first jobs? How happy would you be if you were? I don't know about you, but I don't think being a hostess at El Chico's forever maps onto my values or life goals.

When we label discomfort as bad and therefore something to be avoided, we become increasingly fragile... and fragile things are easy to break. Resilience, strength, and confidence all require us to be uncomfortable at some point. Discomfort is the path to so much of what makes life worthwhile. Might as well view discomfort as a good thing.

I think difficult, different, and discomfort often overlap... and still do not need to be coded as bad. For example, recently Emily, my physical trainer, made me do pull-ups. FIVE SETS. She knows I don't like them. They are difficult. They are different than anything I do in my day-to-day life. And they are hands-down uncomfortable. I have to strain and struggle and push past the point of wanting to quit. I have to work HARD... and I see the value in it. How else am I going to build muscle mass and get stronger? I can't... unless I'm willing to endure—no, *embrace*—"bad" things.

Or how about this one? Having a difficult, uncomfortable conversation with your partner might be different, especially if you or they tend to avoid hard convos, but on the other side lies more understanding and connection. The only way to get there, though, is to go through the difficult discomfort. Think about it, though. What would happen to the quality of our relationships if we could communicate authentically and vulnerably without initiating the this is bad survival sequence (fight-flight-freeze... avoid or escape)?

Continuing in that same vein, therapy and psychedelic experiences can both be difficult. They have the potential to unearth painful emotions, memories, patterns, and realizations. Does that mean these things are bad, to be avoided? Absolutely not. They have the power to be incredibly healing, if not downright transformative.

If we label certain experiences or circumstances as bad when we really mean difficult or uncomfortable, unpleasant or different, then we run the risk of doing ourselves harm on both individual and systemic levels.

IS ANYTHING BAD?

I would argue that *nothing* is inherently good or bad. It completely depends on the context.

Consider pain, for a moment. Is pain good or bad? BAD! Right?

Wait, what about when you're sore after working out? Isn't that a good kind of pain because it means you're getting stronger? Even the pain of grief can be coded as good if you consider that the only way to not feel grief when you lose someone is to have not cared about them at all. Moreover, that pain can be a connection to a lost loved one, a way to still feel their presence. So, pain may be difficult or uncomfortable or unpleasant, but it isn't necessarily bad.

Let's take another admittedly dramatic example to further prove the point. Is murder good or bad?

Knee-jerk reaction is bad, right? But can you think of a circumstance—a context—in which intentionally taking someone's life might actually be for the greater good? I can. Several, in fact. Extreme yes, but it makes the point. Nothing is objectively good or bad. It depends on the context. Therefore, I find it much more helpful to replace "good" and "bad" with more precise words or questions. For example, I routinely talk with my patients about thoughts being *helpful* or *unhelpful*, not good or bad. Is this relationship *healthy* or *unhealthy* for me? Is this goal *aligned with my values* or not? Is this habit *adding to* or *detracting from* my health?

YOUR PSYCH STRENGTH CHALLENGE

As you move forward this week, consider "bad" a red flag. Pay attention to your language, both internal (thoughts) and external (spoken). When you spot that red flag waving at you—and it will—dig in a bit. Be more precise with your language. Describe your experience in more specific detail. *This is hard. This is uncomfortable. This is painful.* Then, and here's the real challenge, see if you can recode it as a good thing. *I want this different/difficult/discomfort/displeasure because...* See what happens when you adjust your mind's default coding.

"There is nothing either good or bad, but thinking makes it so."

—HAMLET in *Hamlet* by William Shakespeare

EVER WONDERED WHY BOTHER? YOU MAY HAVE A CASE OF THE F*CK ITS

I was reading an article about Martin Luther King, Jr. Day, a day marked to honor the influence and inspiration that this man had on our nation. He was, of course, famous for his "I Have a Dream" speech and his fearless advocacy for racial equality. I can't think of MLK without thinking of both the good and the bad. There is the dark side of our country's history (and the ongoing inequalities, inequities, and archaic attitudes that cause pain and stifle growth). In equal measure, Dr. King makes me think of courage, grit, and hope. He embodied these three strengths that represent the best of humanity, and I am in awe of how he continually acted upon the good. I also wonder, as I often do about people who are groundbreaking, earth-shaking, and circumstance-defying, *what* he thought and *how* he thought. What was his mindset? How was he so incredibly resilient?

In addition to MLK Day, the third Monday in January is also known as Blue Monday. Whether it's the gloomy weather, the post-holiday slump, financial worries, or the inevitable waning in New Year, New You motivation, this day can be a hard one. Mental struggles, feeling blue, or full-on depression certainly aren't limited to one day with a catchy marketing name, but it can be a good reminder to pause and think about mental health, the impact that the passing blues or clinical depression can have, and what to do about it.

Somehow these two days coalesced in my mind in a way that made me think of the F*ck Its. I realize that isn't language I typically use in my writing, especially not when I'm wearing the Dr. Ashley hat, but hang in there with me because I'm guessing you can relate.

WHAT ARE THE F*CK ITS?

I love our minds, those powerful yet not always sophisticated frenemies designed to keep us safe but not happy. If you've tuned in to what goes on inside your mind, then you know there are lots of voices inside, lots of habitual thinking patterns or styles of thought processes. At Peak Mind, we call it the Committee in Your Mind, the collection of voices who show up and make commentary on absolutely everything. The voices vie for our attention and control over the one output channel available, our behavior. What that means is that there are lots of thought trains to go down at any given point in time, lots of voices to listen to, and that we can only act on one at a time.

Enter the F*ck Its. This is the line of thinking that sounds something like this:

- *It's not going to work out anyways, so f*ck it.*

- *It doesn't matter, so f*ck it.*

- *It's too hard and I don't have the energy anyways. F*ck it.*

- *The problem is too big to make a dent. F*ck it.*

* *I know I want to [insert big goal here], but [insert more imme-diate want that is going to sabotage your progress] sounds good right now. F*ck it.*

* *The world/my circumstance sucks. F*ck it.*

The formula is usually (something negative that might be abso-lutely true) + (a demand to give up, take the path of least resis-tance, do something self-sabotaging, or slip into despair) = you don't take effective action.

WHERE DO THE F*CK ITS COME FROM?

The F*ck Its can be appealing, sometimes even sounding logical. They are enticing to listen to, especially in the throes of depression when motivation is a rare commodity, the negative filter is on full blast, and hope is low. The depressed mind loves to fall into the F*ck Its because the place it leads to is one that conserves energy. The F*ck Its prevent us from exerting the effort, energy, time, and attention toward something that would be taxing, hard, or scary in some way.

Our minds are master excuse makers, and the F*ck Its is one of the most insidious of the excuse paths.

The F*ck Its show up outside of depression, too, when we're fac-ing circumstances that seem hard in some way. Whether it's an overwhelming situation or something that seems unchangeable, so much bigger than we are that we doubt our ability to make an impact, the F*ck Its show up, again, with the ultimate outcome of making us give up, conserving our mental energy and effort.

Sometimes the F*ck Its arise from a place of anger and self-righ-teous justification. *These circumstances are f-ed up, so f*ck it! I'll do what I want!* Again, there may be some truth to the matter (perhaps the circumstances really *are* bad, unjust, or objectively unfair), but the conclusion is faulty. Giving up or letting the F*ck Its justify you doing something that is actually not in your best interest isn't effective.

WHAT TO DO WITH THE F*CK ITS

As with everything mind-related, it is up to us to develop the psychological strength to make our minds work for us, not against us. The F*ck Its are no different.

Recognize the F*ck Its and call them by name.

Unless we're being mindful or have developed a hefty dose of self-awareness, it's easy to get so wrapped up in what our minds are saying that we don't even realize that we're being pulled down a thought path. It's like we hopped on a train to a destination without even realizing that we're moving and certainly without considering that there were a ton of different trains we could've hopped on.

It's important to get meta here, as in metacognitive. What I mean by that is getting out of the *content* of thinking and looking at the *process* of thinking. The content of thinking refers to the actual words and images that go through our minds. In this case, it's the observation, the negative commentary, and the inevitable F*ck It that follows. In other circumstances, the content may be something like *What if I publish this book, and it flops or offends people?* The actual concerns—flopping and offending—are the *content* of thinking. The *process*, however, is worry. That is a worry thought, which, as you know, is an anticipation of a potential problem.

Here's another example. *This isn't my best writing.* The statement about my writing, that's the *content*. The *process* (or type of thinking) is judgment.

It's their fault the world is in this state is content. Blaming is process.

I'll never get this done is content. Prediction is process.

Chocolate and vanilla are content. Ice cream or even dessert are process. Does that make sense?

One of the most effective ways to get out of the unhelpful content is by simply labeling the type of thinking process that is happening. It gives you some mental distance from the thought, keeps you from getting tangled up in it, and helps you realize that you don't have to treat it as capital-T-Truth because there's a good chance it isn't.

Take a minute a get clear on what the F*ck Its sound like for you so that when they show up, you can play I spy. *I see what you're doing there, Mind. That's just the F*ck Its!*

Don't get bogged down in whether it's true or objective. Focus on whether it's helpful.

This is, perhaps, the most important realization we can have: just because we are having a thought does not mean that it is true, important, meaningful, or worth listening to. Thinking is just what our minds do, and a lot of the thoughts they produce are just noise. Useless noise.

Learning to ask whether or not a thought is *helpful* to listen to is a critical skill. It's like learning which friends to listen to when you need advice. If you have a friend who always blows things out of proportion, expects the worst, or is overly indulgent, that's not the friend you go to for advice and encouragement when you're really wanting to make a good decision or move toward a goal. Same thing here. A lot of those voices in our head, those Committee Members, are not good friends. They are naysay, path of least resistance, don't put yourself out there voices. From this point on, no matter how loud or real they *feel*, if they're not *helpful*, they get disregarded.

Only act on helpful thoughts.

Remember the game Simon Says from childhood? The premise of the game is that "Simon" gives directions and you must decide whether to follow them or not. (In the game, you only follow the instructions that start with "Simon says....") Simon tries to trick you into following the commands you shouldn't, and then you lose!

Sometimes psychological strength is just a more grown-up version of Simon Says. If your mind tells you something (like *F*ck it, don't go to the gym. F*ck it, don't advocate for change. F*ck it, sleep in. F*ck it, keep your feelings to yourself. F*ck it, whatever*) that isn't helpful, your job is to disregard it completely. Simon didn't say jump. Don't jump!

The bottom line is that just because we think something, even if it feels completely real, true, and meaningful, we absolutely do not have to act on it. This is the only way I know to get out of the F*ck Its. Do it anyways, *even if your mind is screaming that it's pointless, it won't make a difference, or you just can't.* The reality is, you probably can, it might make a difference, especially if you do it over and over again, and there very well may be a point to it, if nothing else the point being that you're the kind of person who does XYZ.

WHEN THE F*CK ITS ARE HELPFUL

In the interest of being thorough, I want to acknowledge that there are times when the F*ck It mentality might actually be helpful, which is why the *Is this helpful or not?* evaluation is such a critical step.

If I want to, say, be a writer, then listening to the voice that says F*ck It might be helpful if it leads me to override self-doubt or fear. For example, one Committee Member might say, "You can't come up with ideas as creative as Brandon Sanderson (the best fiction author out there, in my humble, yet strong, opinion). You'll never be able to write an epic fantasy novel." Sounds pretty true to me, but that's *content*. What's *process*? Comparisons and predictions.

Is it helpful? No. Not if I really want to write a fantasy novel.

If I can tap into the F*ck Its in the sense of *What do I have to lose? F*ck It*, I just might be willing to put in the time and effort to brainstorm and try my hand at creative writing. If the F*ck Its help you be brave and willing to take chances or do the work, then, by all means, listen to them! If, however, they're taking you down the path of defeat, despair, self-sabotage, inertia, or stuckness, say f*ck it to the F*ck Its and defy them! Do the thing they're trying to prevent you from doing. You'll thank yourself later.

---

*"F*ck it can help you or harm you."*

—ICE T

THINK LIKE A SCIENTIST: USING EXPERIMENTATION TO ENHANCE YOUR LIFE

Do you consider yourself a scientist? Maybe you're not a whatever-ologist and maybe you've never worked in a research lab, but I want to make the case for approaching life like a scientist because a little experimentation can go a long way in enhancing your life.

Real scientists don't just say, "I know what's going to happen." Instead, they use the scientific method to empirically test out their theories. The scientific method is all about testing a hypothesis or prediction by gathering data. They design experiments, run them, and see what happens. Then, they draw conclusions based on their *data*, not their hunches or assumptions. I believe we can—and should—do the same thing in our lives. That's why I implore you to embrace an experimental mindset.

AN EXPERIMENTAL MINDSET

So, what exactly is an experimental mindset? It's the recognition that we're not that great at predicting things, the belief that direct experience is the most effective and reliable teacher, and a willingness to try things out.

According to Oxford, experimentation is the "action or process of trying out new ideas, methods, or activities." What a great way to go through life!

Every time you try something new, you gather data in the form of your direct experience. Do it repeatedly, and you may start to see a pattern emerge, allowing you to draw conclusions... and the conclusions may surprise you.

As an intern at Children's Mercy Hospital way back when, I was incredibly excited about my rotation in Consultation/Liaison services. These services involved visiting the various hospital floors, at the request of other medical team members, to provide psychological assessments, interventions, or recommendations. I just KNEW I was going to love being in the hospital and working in integrated medical teams.

Except that I didn't.

What I "knew" was really just a prediction and, thankfully, one I was forced to test out by my training program. The several months I spent doing C/L weren't my favorite. I found out, through my direct experience, that I don't love the one-and-done interactions of consults. I prefer the ongoing relationship aspect of therapy. I also didn't like the unpredictability of consult requests coming through, sometimes just minutes before I was planning to pack up and head home. In short, it wasn't my jam, but I wouldn't have known without experiencing it.

WHO DO YOU TRUST?

Our minds are designed to make predictions about what's going to happen. They recognize patterns, operate on assumptions, and draw conclusions based on those patterns and assumptions.

In other words, our minds offer their best, albeit biased, guesses about what the future holds.

Our minds tend to skew negative, so those predictions and assumptions aren't generally the most optimistic, let alone accurate. They are the product of shortcuts our minds take in processing information and the creative license they take to fill in gaps and keep us safe. One of those shortcuts and creative liberties is the confirmation bias.

Our minds actually filter out a lot of information, completely disregarding it as though it didn't even exist. Think of a teenager who is nodding and pretending to listen to their parent's lecture, only really tuning in when they hear, "Are you even listening?" Everything else is in one ear and out the other. Our minds do the same thing, filtering out information that doesn't fit with our beliefs or assumptions or stuff that otherwise seems irrelevant.

Our minds jump to conclusions, and we tend to take them at their word... even though their hit rate is actually pretty low. How many times have you been convinced that something was going to be awful only to find yourself pleasantly surprised? We're about as good at predicting how we're going to feel (called affective forecasting) as my weather app is at predicting the weather. (0% chance of rain today, huh? Then, why am I getting wet on my walk home?)

It's not just predicting how we're going to feel, either. We're pretty off base when it comes to anticipating how events are going to unfold, what impact something will have on us, and what we're actually capable of.

Our minds lie to us all the time.

If I had a friend who told me as many factually untrue or categorically unhelpful things as my mind does, let's just say I would take everything that friend said with a grain of salt... if we even stayed friends. Yet, we fall for our mind's propaganda all the time.

Rather than trusting what we *think*, we should trust what we *experience*. Trust your five senses—what you see, hear, smell, taste, and feel—and perhaps your emotions (though there are times when our emotions aren't to be trusted, either).

That brings us back to experimentation.

EXPERIMENTATION

Several years ago, when I was first starting to dabble in life design and intentional experimentation, I decided to do 30 days without watching TV. I didn't really have a hypothesis I was testing. Rather, it was more of a curiosity. Could I do it (I was a big TV watcher)? And if so, what would it be like?

After 30 days, I learned two things. One, yes, I can go without watching TV, which means I can start and stop habits. And two, my sleep improved, which was a surprise to me. I've never had a TV in my bedroom, so I didn't connect those two dots. Still, my direct experience—my data—clearly showed that I got better, more consistent sleep when TV wasn't a part of my routine. Interesting.

In the years since then, I find myself running experiments all the time. Some are lifestyle:

* What would intermittent fasting feel like in my body? (Turns out, it works well for me.)

* What would working out with a trainer do for me? (I committed to 10 sessions... and was hooked. Strength noticeably increased, and I dread working out a whole lot less.)

* What will happen if I implement a screen curfew? (I sleep better.)

Some are relational:

* What difference will it make if I text people as soon as I think of them, for no reason other than I'm thinking of them? (So far, I feel more connected and less lonely.)

* What happens if I'm more vulnerable? (I feel super uncomfortable, but also strangely more confident, and there's less second-guessing, overanalyzing, or unnecessary strife.)

Some are business:

* Can ChatGPT write better cold email copy than I can? (Jury's still out as both of our response rates are abysmal.)

* Will allowing my patients to schedule online make things easier or harder? (Easier, for sure, in the sense of cutting down on back-and-forth emails. Added bonus? It's a lot easier to stick with my scheduling boundaries and work my desired hours.)

I experiment with leisure, in the kitchen, with professional identity, and methods for styling curly hair. You name it. If it can be tested or modified or explored, it's fair game.

THE BENEFITS OF AN EXPERIMENTAL MINDSET

I am 100% sold on the value of an experimental mindset, based on my own—you guessed it—direct experience. It's an approach to life that turns the pressure down and feels more forgiving and playful.

Approaching a change as an experiment makes it feel more doable. There's less fear of failure because you can't fail an experiment. You simply gather data, course correct based on those data, and run a new experiment.

It also takes down the fear of change. For example, in 2022, I decided to switch my psychology practice to a fully virtual one. I was pretty sure that would be a good move for me, but I was scared. *What if I regret it? What if I lose a lot of patients? What if I end up being a hermit and never leaving my house?* All of the what ifs, which, as you know, are just code for worry. I knew that, too, but it was still hard to make the leap.

Thinking of it as an experiment—*I'll try this for six months then reassess*—made it feel more tenable. It was a change I was more willing to embrace, so that mindset was helpful and effective because it kept me from being stuck. I ran the experiment, and six months later, gave up my office because I didn't see going back.

Experimenting—trying something out knowing that you are not committing to it forever or strictly invested in a particular outcome—can be freeing. It offers more space to try things. It offers more protection when things don't turn out well. You didn't fail. You didn't make a mistake. You ran an experiment, gathered your data, and learned something valuable.

YOUR CHALLENGE

My challenge to you, dear friend, is to approach life like a scientist. Embrace an experimental mindset and start dabbling with experimentation. To jumpstart things, ask yourself these questions:

* What experiments can you test out?

* Where can you start to challenge your mind's assumptions?

* Where can you start to really listen to and trust your experience rather than your thoughts?

Try it out, see what happens, and decide if it's worth continuing. What do you have to lose?

"What works for one artist doesn't necessarily work for another; try anything and everything and go with what works for you."

—PAUL DIXON

The Way I See It

SECTION 2

Wrangling Emotions

L ike it or not, we all have emotions—a full range of both positive and negative ones—and we need them. They give us important information and guide our decisions. Of course, they can also wreak havoc in our lives if we let them.

Sometimes we're flooded by strong emotions. They take over, and we are left reeling and cleaning up the mess that our messy feelings made. On the other end of the spectrum, we suppress our feelings. Shove them down. Distract. Numb. Drink. Eat your feelings. Avoid. Escape. Bottle it up until you blow.

We need another option. When it comes to our emotions, we need to heed their guidance but not be ruled by them. We need to be able to name them, to accurately know what we're feeling and why, but that's a surprisingly difficult thing to do, thanks, in part, to all of the misinformation out there. *Don't feel that way. That feeling is bad. You're too sensitive. You're being emotional.*

We're not really taught what is normal when it comes to feelings and what to do with them when they show up. It's no wonder that so many people have a dysfunctional relationship with their emotions. The good news is that this relationship can be repaired. You can learn to navigate your feelings with strength and wisdom.

STOP FEELING BAD

How many times have you said, "I feel bad"? How many times have you been asked "What's wrong?" or told "Don't be sad/mad/worried/_____?" About a million, right? And therein lies a problem.

We are taught from early on that certain emotions are good. They're okay to have. They are desired. Other emotions, in contrast, are bad. We shouldn't want them, or worse, we shouldn't even have them. We're taught to believe that when they show up, there's something wrong. There's a problem—our EMOTIONS are a problem—and problems need to be fixed. This leads to working hard to get rid of those "bad" feelings. Unfortunately, avoiding, suppressing, getting rid of, or otherwise fixing feelings doesn't actually work. Worse, we might even pile on to them by beating ourselves up for having them in the first place.

What most people aren't taught is that emotions—the *full range* of emotions—are normal and natural. By virtue of being human, you are destined to feel sad. And mad. And guilty, jealous, joyful, embarrassed, confident, ashamed, happy, disheartened, peaceful, confused, surprised, ambivalent, horrified, empty, excited, etc. You will feel them all, whether you want to or not. In fact, we're wired to have twice as many negative emotions as positive ones, and we have them for a reason.

EMOTIONS SERVE AN EVOLUTIONARY PURPOSE

Our brains have the enormous job of processing every bit of data coming in through our five senses every second of the day so that they can keep us alive. That's a lot to sift through and make sense of, so they've developed a lot of shortcuts. Emotions are one.

Emotions are messengers designed to give us a lot of information very quickly and motivate us to act in certain ways, aimed at ensuring our survival.

Think about it. The message of anxiety is danger, and the action urge is to avoid or escape. That's very helpful when a threat to our bodily safety is near. The message of guilt is I did something wrong, and the urge is to make amends. Again, helpful for a social species whose survival depended on being part of the community. Even in present day, when we're not likely to be eaten by predators or die if we are shunned, emotions are incredibly useful... when we understand and have a healthy relationship with them.

REDEFINING YOUR RELATIONSHIP

Bad is not feeling. Neither is good. Those are judgments, another brain shortcut. Our brains quickly categorize things as good and bad, safe and unsafe, desired or undesired to speed up information processing. When it comes to feelings, though, judging them is part of the problem. That's not promoting a healthy relationship with them. Consider this. How healthy is your relationship with that person who constantly judges you?

When we designate natural, normal experiences as "bad," we're setting ourselves up to struggle. Feeling sad or anxious or angry or guilty at some point is unavoidable. (Remember, we are literally wired to feel them.) Yet, when we call something "bad," we are saying to ourselves that we shouldn't have that experience, that there is something inherently wrong with what's going on inside of us. That would be like saying that having to go to the bathroom or eat or sleep is bad. It's just a part of being human. We accept those experiences, throughout the course of our day, and move on.

We need to do the same with feelings

When we can learn to recognize the emotions that show up and call them by their proper names, not "good" or "bad," with the understanding that they are there for a reason, we are now open to receiving their messages. From there, we can decide whether the message is helpful or not and whether to act on the accompanying urge or override it.

DEALING WITH PAINFUL EMOTIONS

Once we are able to pause, take a step back, and call our emotion by its name, we've already begun to make space for it, to allow it to be there. As we examine our emotion with curiosity, we can reflect on whether acting on it is in our best interest. The goal is to take the input from your feelings under consideration but to stay in the driver's seat of your actions. And sometimes the best course of action, the one that keeps you moving in the direction that is right for you, is simply to be patient.

All emotions, even the most intense and difficult ones, will pass if we let them. If we do not add fuel to the fire and, instead, know that we won't drown in them if we just stay mindful and compassionate, they will burn out.

I heard this quote the other day that so deeply resonated: "Emotions are not math problems to be solved. They are sunsets to be experienced."

If that didn't immediately make you pause, read it again.

That shift in perspective leads to a fundamentally different way of relating to your emotions, a new way to be with them, especially the unpleasant ones. It allows you to make space for and explore with curiosity the very human experience of emotions.

Instead of judging feelings and falling into the trap that comes from having "bad" feelings, we need to accurately recognize them and precisely name them, open ourselves up to having them so that we can explore them with curiosity, glean their message, then move forward intentionally. We need to bask in those sunsets.

"Emotions are not math problems to be solved.
They are sunsets to be experienced."

—DR. ROBYN WALSER

DEALING WITH UNDESERVED GUILT

I cannot tell you how many people I encounter—in my psychology practice, through my work with Peak Mind, and just in life in general—who are guilt-y.

I don't mean guilty of some crime or faux pas. Rather, *guilt-y* as in prone to experiencing excessive guilt.

This is you if:

* You frequently feel "bad," especially about something you did or didn't do.

* You apologize at the drop of a hat.

* You still feel "bad" even after you've apologized or made amends.

* You find yourself saying or thinking *I should've* or *I shouldn't have* with any regularity.

* You can't forgive yourself or let go of past transgressions, especially ones that are relatively minor.

THE PURPOSE OF GUILT

Guilt, as with all emotions, serves an evolutionary purpose. Emotions are a shortcut way for our brains to quickly convey a lot of information and guidance on how to proceed in a given situation. The message of guilt is that I did something wrong, and the directive is to make amends or repair things.

From an evolutionary perspective, guilt served the purpose of keeping us in line. Humans were designed as communal creatures. Cavemen and women couldn't survive on their own. Therefore, if they did something egregious to upset the herd and got kicked out, death was a likely outcome.

Enter guilt, which helped us recognize when we misstepped so we could fix it, continue as part of the community, and, ultimately, stay alive.

Guilt can be a powerful tool for learning and growth. Because it's a pretty unpleasant experience, it can be an effective teacher, guiding us to operate within our personal code of ethics and values and to interact with others effectively. Guilt can be very handy... and it can be a source of misery.

WHEN GUILT GOES WRONG

I tend to primarily hear about two flavors of undeserved guilt. The first arises when people feel guilty for doing something that isn't actually wrong or bad. We *should* feel guilty when we do something wrong. What constitutes wrong, however, is up for debate.

Let's agree that wrong means something that causes harm. Do you experience guilt in the absence of harm? And what actually qualifies as harm?

Take, for example, saying no to someone. Is the act of saying no morally wrong? No. Does it cause damage or harm? No. (In fact, I might argue that *not* saying no can actually cause damage or harm.)

Do others like hearing no? Not necessarily, but their displeasure, disappointment, or frustration does not mean that you did anything wrong. Moreover, negative feelings are not harmful anyways, contrary to popular opinion. Others' emotional responses are either a reflection of natural human emotion and/or their responsibility to manage. Keep in mind that disappointment is a natural feeling that arises when reality does not match our expectations. Someone being disappointed when you say no means that reality did not match their expectations. That. Is. It. You are not responsible for other people's expectations or emotions.

Let's extend this a bit, too. If YOU are experiencing emotions, even difficult or unwanted ones, are YOU doing something wrong? No, of course not. So, why do we amplify our emotional distress by believing that we shouldn't be feeling that way, that there's something wrong with us for having that emotional experience? That's just piling on undeserved guilt.

Does doing normal human things or meeting your own needs mean you did something wrong? Think about it. Do you feel guilty when you need to ask for help? When you engage in a little self-care? Lots of people do, unfortunately. Yet that does not mean that the guilt is deserved. Needing help and taking care of yourself are so utterly human and, arguably *good* things, not bad.

And what about making mistakes? Should we feel guilty when we make a mistake? Maybe, under certain circumstances, I suppose. But that's with the caveat that you're not approaching mistakes in a black-or-white, all-or-none kind of way. All mistakes are not created equal. Perhaps most mistakes are innocent, meaning that most people would make the same one either because of a learning curve or human error. Not all mistakes result in any sort of harm. So, even if it was a careless, preventable mistake, it's not worth the guilt if there wasn't even a negative outcome. (Again, keeping in mind that someone being disappointed or angry doesn't count as a negative outcome. Now, if they are *hurt* by your actions, that warrants more exploration.)

The second flavor of undeserved guilt I see frequently is the guilt that stems from a sense of over-responsibility, which is when you take on too big a slice of the responsibility pie. If someone you care about is really struggling, you may feel "bad." That "bad" often gets categorized as guilt, but it's an error. Did you cause their suffering? Are you actually responsible for it? Is there even anything you can actually do to alleviate it for them? If the answers are no, then dig into the feeling a little more. You're defaulting to guilt when the actual emotion may be something like sympathy, compassion, or pity.

GETTING PAST THE GUILT

How can you release yourself from the shackles of unnecessary guilt? First and foremost, you must appropriately identify your emotions. This is the foundation of emotional intelligence and a critical component of psychological strength. In this case, that means doing two things.

1. **REMEMBER THAT "BAD" IS NOT A FEELING.** It's a judgment. If you find yourself feeling "bad," ask yourself what flavor of bad. If the answer is guilt, then...

2. **CHECK THE FACTS.** Did you actually do something wrong? Did that wrong thing result in harm to someone or something?

If you're experiencing justifiable guilt, then make amends. Take steps to rectify the situation and to repair the relationship that was damaged. If, however, what you are experiencing is excessive or undeserved guilt, then you've got some work to do.

Get a hold of your beliefs. It's not always as easy as just deciding to think something else, but it is absolutely possible to change unhelpful beliefs. Remind yourself (a million times a day or until it feels like truth) that:

* Doing something that upsets someone else does not mean that what you did was wrong.

* Taking care of yourself is not wrong or harmful.

* Saying no is not wrong.

Once you're at least starting to get on board with the idea that your guilt system may be a little sensitive or may tend to dump a disproportionate amount of guilt on you, then you can really start to break free from its binds.

STOP APOLOGIZING. If you've done something wrong, by all means, give a good, sincere apology (one that acknowledges what you did, takes responsibility, acknowledges the impact on the other person, and expresses sincere regret or remorse). Then stop. One heartfelt apology is probably enough. And don't even apologize once for normal human things like existing or taking up space.

> **PRO TIP:** If you really feel like you need to apologize and keeping your mouth shut is too hard, switch it to a thank you instead. "I'm sorry that I'm a few minutes late" becomes "Thank you for your patience."

BAN THE WORD SHOULD FROM YOUR VOCABULARY, INTERNALLY AND SPOKEN OUT LOUD. "Shoulds" lead to guilt (or anger or anxiety), implying that you did something wrong when, in fact, you probably didn't. Just because it could be done differently does not mean that it was wrong.

PULL OUT YOUR MINDFULNESS SKILLS. Mindfulness means paying attention, on purpose, to the present. In other words, it's focusing on what you're doing or experiencing here and now. If you find yourself still feeling guilty over things that happened eons ago or things that you have already repaired, then the work to be done is to stop the rumination and mental self-flagellation. Whether you realize it or not, rumination is a habit. It may seem to happen naturally or involuntarily, but it is something that you can exercise control over.

Just like stopping nail biting, a pesky habit, you must recognize when you are doing it then decide to stop and engage in something else. When you notice your mind rehashing old territory for the umpteenth time, decide to stop and fully focus your attention on something else.

IF THE GUILT IS ACTUALLY ANOTHER DISPLACED EMOTION, SEE IF YOU CAN GET CLEARER ON WHAT YOU ARE ACTUALLY FEELING AND WHY. Then, navigate that emotion with psychological strength. What might that feeling be telling you? Is it a message worth listening to? Is it accurate and helpful in this situation? Is there anything you need to or can do? Or, is it something you need to just sit with? How can you make space for that difficult emotion? How can you be kind to yourself in this hard moment?

YOUR CHEAT SHEET

One of my favorite fast techniques for reducing undeserved guilt (or coping with any hard experience, really) is called a Self-Compassion Break. Developed by psychologist Dr. Kristin Neff, a leading voice in the area of self-compassion, this 5-minute exercise works wonders. You can download my version for free at www.drashleysmith.com/the-way-I-see-it-tools.

Stop letting your mind take you on undeserved guilt trips. There are so many other, more joyful places to go instead!

"Guilt is cancer. Guilt will confine you, torture you, destroy you as an artist. It's a black wall. It's a thief."

—DAVE GROHL

LETTING GO OF REGRETS

R egret is a funny thing. It can be incredibly painful, yet informative, or a colossal waste of time. It can be a source of growth and motivation, or it can be an anchor that keeps us stuck in the past. Either way, letting go of regret is important for moving forward.

Do you have any regrets? I assume at least one or two because, I mean, who doesn't? But, more importantly, what is your *relationship* with regret?

I don't know how anyone could make it through life without the *potential* for regret. We will inevitably say or do something that, in hindsight, we wish we hadn't. Or we will realize, too late, that we missed an opportunity and left something important unsaid or undone. Those kinds of things happen in all of our lives, yet the way we respond to those regrets can be very different. For some, regret is consuming while others make peace with the past and find a path forward.

RECOGNIZING REGRET WITH EMOTIONAL INTELLIGENCE

As with all emotions, regret serves a purpose. It gives us a message. Regret tells us that we need to look at our actions because they may be causing problems or aren't in line with who we really are. That can be important information to heed if it 1) is justified and 2) prompts reflection and change.

Is This Regret Justified?

Sometimes we experience regret that isn't really deserved or justified because we didn't actually do anything wrong. We didn't make a mistake. It's a regret false alarm, if you will, that arises from our underlying thinking.

Belief: There are right and wrong decisions.

It's tempting to judge the quality of our past decisions by their outcomes, but that's based on faulty logic. Sometimes you can make the right decision at the time based on the available information, but statistics take over. We play the odds, but there are no guarantees. Lightning strikes sometimes.

You can eat healthy and still get heart disease. Does that mean you should regret your lifestyle?

You can take a new job, realize that you don't like it, and make another change. Does that mean you shouldn't have taken that job? Not necessarily. It's possible that the "regrettable" decision of taking that job is actually the springboard to something truly fulfilling.

You tell the truth and hurt someone's feelings. Sure, you might wish they weren't in pain, but does that mean you should take back your words if you could? Again, not necessarily.

Belief: Doing something differently would have led to a better outcome.

Humans are wired to recognize cause and effect. That's a really useful thing... except when it may not be accurate. We often believe that if we could have done something differently it would have led to a different and better outcome. That seems logical. But it may not be.

Let's say you lost track of time and were late for work and got written up. It's easy to feel regretful, to entertain the idea of *If only I had gotten up earlier or not gotten online in the morning or my kid hadn't had a meltdown, I wouldn't have gotten in trouble at work.* Yes, it's quite possible that if you had done things differently in the morning you would've been on time to work and not gotten written up. It's also quite possible that you would've gotten stuck in traffic and still ended up late, or that you would've gotten to the intersection just as another driver blew through a red light and ended up in a car accident. There's no way to know.

Rethinking Regret

We need to question regret when it shows up to see if it's something we need to listen to. Maybe it's not that our actions were questionable but rather a reflection of being in a tough situation now. We need to dig in a bit and get clear on what we're really feeling. And we need to remember that right decisions do not guarantee desired outcomes. In fact, there may not even be a right decision. This is an interesting perspective to take and one that can lead to compassion and appreciation for your Past Self, rather than undeserved criticism and judgment.

COPING WITH REAL REGRETS

Let's say, though, that you aren't falling into logical fallacies or being undeservedly critical of your Past Self. What about those times when you really did do or say something that was unskilled or hurtful or directly led to something bad? When that regret is justified, when it's there to tell you, "Hey, you messed up." Then what?

Regret tells us to examine our actions. That's worth doing if we can do it in an effective way. Reflect. Understand what you did (or didn't) do and the impact those actions had. Explore why you made that decision at the time so you can understand your motives. Take responsibility for what you need to. Take away a useful lesson to guide you in the future so that you can act with integrity and courage and be the person you want to be. Then, move forward.

GETTING PAST REGRET WHEN YOU'RE STUCK IN THE PAST

Problems arise when, instead of listening to regret and moving forward, we get stuck in the past on an endless loop of rumination. *If only I hadn't... If only I had... instead.*

It's tempting to go down the if only path, but what lies at the end of it?

Nothing.

Because there is no end. It becomes a loop, our minds going round and round revising history, rehashing the same territory with no new insights. Besides the fact that we can't go back in time and have a do over, rumination, regardless of the focus, is a pretty toxic mental habit. It keeps us out of the present and prevents us from taking meaningful, effective action.

So, why do we do it?

When it comes to regret, sometimes we ruminate because we don't really know a more skillful way for coping with the pain. Sometimes it's because we're holding on to some unhelpful beliefs. Sometimes it's just a bad habit. And sometimes it's a form of self-punishment. Regardless of the reason, it's time to let it go and stop ruminating.

LETTING GO OF REGRETS

When your mind is pulling you down that if only path. Go down it. Once. Take an objective look at what happened and why you did (or didn't do) that. Learn what you need to in order to move forward. *I wish I had _____ instead because _____. Here's what I'll do next time.* Then, work on having compassion for and forgiving your Past Self.

It's tempting to revise history in your imagination, but it's not helpful. You can't go back and change it, and mentally trying to fix it keeps you from moving forward.

"We should regret our mistakes and learn from them, but never carry them into the future with us."

—LUCY MAUD MONTGOMERY

ANXIETY AND THE BRAIN

I t goes by many names: anxiety, worry, nervousness, panic, discomfort, unease, apprehension, self-consciousness, insecurity, doubt, fear. Whatever you call it, this experience is unpleasant, to say the least.

Whether you have normative anxiety (meaning natural, it's just the way humans work) or a full-blown anxiety disorder, every single one of us will feel anxious at some point. Many times, it goes beyond just making us a little uncomfortable and becomes so overwhelming or aversive that it stops us in our tracks, preventing us from leading the kinds of lives we long for. That's why the more we know about anxiety, the better.

WHY DO WE HAVE ANXIETY?

Anxiety is our body's built in warning system, designed to detect—and prevent—potential threats. It's what keeps us safe.

Our minds are essentially pattern recognition software, and when they pick up on some sort of indication that a possible bad thing could happen to us, our fight-or-flight system gets activated (hello, anxiety!), with the goal of helping us escape or avoid the danger. It is one of the most primitive circuits in our brains. *And. It. Is. Powerful.*

But what's really going on inside our brains? Allow me to introduce The Caveman and The CEO.

THE CAVEMAN AND THE CEO

Our brains are made up of tons of interconnected parts that work together. For our purposes, we're going to simplify things a bit and focus on two specific parts, the stars of our emotion center and our logic center, respectively.

The Amygdala

The star of our emotion center (called the limbic system for my fellow brain nerds) is a little almond-shaped guy called the amygdala. (Technically, we have two, one on each side, but go with me.) I like to think of the amygdala as The Caveman.

The Caveman is incredibly powerful... but not very sophisticated. It doesn't speak English, which is why we can't reason with it. We'll come back to that in a minute...

The Caveman simply labels things as good or bad, safe or unsafe. There's no nuance or in between. When something happens that is bad or unsafe in some way, The Caveman makes note of it.

It also makes note of anything associated with the bad thing. Think of it like connecting the dots. *This is bad. This is like that bad thing, so this is bad, too. This is also like that, so it's bad.* Anything that is similar in any way gets coded as bad. These associations aren't always apparently logical, either. Sometimes dots get connected just because they happen around the same time (like a doctor's white coat getting associated with a painful shot).

Because our brains like to recognize patterns, anything even remotely connected to or associated with the bad thing gets lumped into the pattern... whether we consciously realize it or not. Ever felt anxious for no discernible reason? Your Caveman picked up on something coded as bad—some sight, smell, taste, sound, or sensation, some tiny part of a pattern—then did its thing: it sounded the alarm.

The Prefrontal Cortex

The CEO (our prefrontal cortex) is the seat of our logic and reason. This is the part of our brain that does what's called executive functioning. It's the part that can deliberately think things through and anticipate possible outcomes, which means it can analyze and conclude that we might be in danger. If you've ever gone down the *what if* path and ended up at a place of anxiety, your CEO got you there.

The CEO is more sophisticated, more capable of nuance, but it takes more time and effort to do its job than The Caveman. In part, that's because of how close they are to Grand Central Station.

The Thalamus

Any information coming into our brain goes to the thalamus first, which I think of as Grand Central Station (GCS). GCS processes all incoming data, packages it up, and sends it out for review and instructions on what to do. It sends the info to both The Caveman and The CEO, and both process it for signs of danger.

The thing is, those packages get to The Caveman first. It's a closer stop to Grand Central Station, if you will. If The Caveman detects any hint of anything coded bad/unsafe... Alarm bells. Anxiety. Game over. The CEO doesn't even get a chance to weigh in.

If The Caveman doesn't go off immediately, The CEO has a chance to take a look at the package and think things through. If The CEO figures out that this information could be foreshadowing danger, threat, or some other negative outcome, guess what it does... it stamps it BAD and sends it to The Caveman, where The Caveman does its thing: Label it. Connect dots. Set off alarm bells. Anxiety. Game over.

HOW DO WE DEAL WITH ANXIETY?

Understanding that there are two pathways to anxiety and knowing the key players and how they work sheds light on things we can do to override and rewire our anxiety systems.

CALMING THE CEO

With a solid foundation in place, you're ready to actually start training your brain to be less anxious. The CEO is the part of your brain that *thinks* your way into anxiety by anticipating negative outcomes. Therefore, one of the most effective CEO-based strategies is rational thinking.

If you understand that our brains are wired toward negativity AND that they take shortcuts to speed up their information processing, then you know that you can't believe everything you think.

Learn to pause and question your automatic thoughts. Recognize when you're jumping to conclusions and expecting the worst. Then, ask yourself key questions like:

* Where's the evidence for and against this thought?

* Do I know this for sure?

* What are three other possible explanations or outcomes?

* What's the realistic worst thing that could happen? Could I handle it?

* So, what if... will it really matter in a week, a month, or a year?

Recognizing your thoughts, questioning whether they are both accurate AND helpful, then reframing them to be more realistic is a technique called cognitive restructuring or thought challenging. It takes a lot of practice, but it's a powerful tool for minimizing anxiety. That said, in my experience, rational thinking is a 50/50 thing. That's because a lot of anxiety is driven by The Caveman.

TAMING THE CAVEMAN

Remember how I said The Caveman doesn't speak English? What I mean is that it operates outside of our logic and language, so you can't just ask it, "What's going on, Caveman?" and you can't just tell it, "Chill out, dude. We're fine." You can't reason with it. Instead, you have two main tactics: relaxation and exposure.

Relaxation

Relaxation strategies like deep belly breathing and progressive muscle relaxation (systematically tightening and relaxing your muscles one by one—just google "progressive muscle relaxation" for tons of guided options) can help settle your Caveman.

Relaxation strategies work by activating your parasympathetic nervous system, the branch that is responsible for countering your fight-or-flight system. Keep in mind that one deep breath is not going to erase anxiety, but with practice, you can help calm your anxiety response.

Exposure

This is hands down THE most effective strategy for training your brain to be less anxious. Think of exposure as facing your fears.

When you listen to your Caveman by avoiding or escaping the situations it deems bad—that is, when you treat the resulting anxiety as a true alarm instead of a false alarm—you're actually reinforcing the anxiety. You're basically saying, "Good job, Caveman! Keep it up!" And you are all but guaranteeing more anxiety in the future.

Instead, with exposure, you're doing the complete opposite. You essentially take your Caveman into a situation that it deems bad or unsafe. It's going to freak out, sounding the alarms and triggering anxiety. Then—and this is the key—you hang out in the situation, using your *actions* to show your brain that there is no real threat and that it can chill out.

Exposure is one of those "actions speak louder than words" and "experience is the best teacher" kind of situations. We have to show our Caveman that it has it wrong. Over time and with repetition, our Cavemen learn, and they will recode the situation as not bad.

MINDFULNESS

Our other powerhouse of a tool for quieting anxiety is mindfulness. Simply put, mindfulness is training your attention to focus on the present moment without judgment. Mindfulness helps quiet anxiety produced by both our Cavemen and CEOs. It does double duty!

When The Caveman pipes up, The CEO literally goes offline (part of the reason you can't logic away anxiety). Mindfulness not only helps The Caveman calm down, but it also helps strengthen the mental muscle that pulls The CEO back online.

Pair exposure WITH mindfulness and you'll have a one-two punch ready to knock anxiety nearly out.

"Each of us must confront our own fears, must come face to face with them. How we handle our fears will determine where we go with the rest of our lives. To experience adventure or to be limited by the fear of it."

—JUDY BLUME

HOW TO DEAL WITH DISAPPOINTMENT

Disappointment is a part of life. From being let down by relatively inconsequential things like a series finale or the outcome of the latest football game to major pain points like finding out your person isn't who you thought they were, the sting of disappointment is familiar.

Whichever side of it you're on—the one who is disappoint*ed* or the one who is disappoint*ing*—it's not fun.

So, how do we deal with inevitable disappointment? Let's get right to it.

WHAT IS DISAPPOINTMENT?

Like all emotions, disappointment is simply a shortcut from our brain designed to give us a message. The message of disappointment? Reality does not match my expectations... in a way I don't like. We feel disappointed when we thought one thing was going to happen—that it *should* happen in a certain way—but it didn't.

And as with all emotions, sometimes the message is important. We need to listen to it and use it to inform our actions. Other times, however, it's bogus. Spam. A false alarm. Unnecessary inside "ick."

Differentiating when a feeling is meaningful and when it isn't is important.

THE ROLE OF EXPECTATIONS

The heart of disappointment is really unmet expectations, which raises the critical issue of what's the real problem here. Is the problem reality? What someone did or didn't do or the way things turned out? Or does the problem lie with the expectations themselves?

There's the old debate of whether it's better to set your expectations low and be pleasantly surprised or set them high and run the risk of being disappointed. You can make a case for either, but I'd argue that not setting expectations at all is more ideal.

When we can let go of expectations, what we're really doing is not placing any demands on the future. Instead, we're exercising a powerful mindfulness move and allowing things to unfold as they are. Without expectations, we are more open to experience, less prone to judgment, and protected against disappointment. Thus, one way to deal with disappointment is simply to not have expectations.

While I believe that we'd experience far less disappointment if we held far fewer expectations, I don't think it's realistic to go through life expectation-free. I doubt we probably should even if we could.

Sometimes expectations are what keep us safe and secure. Mutually agreed upon and upheld expectations—for example, that I will be there for you and you will be there for me or if I show up for work you will pay me for the work I do—allow us to form trust within relationships.

Expectations about how the world works allow us to stay committed to long-term goals; I expect that if I graduate from school, I'll have more job opportunities or that if I save for retirement, my Future Self will be taken care of. Expectations aren't all bad, but they are the driver of disappointment.

So, then, when we experience disappointment, is it an internal or external issue?

WHAT TO DO WHEN YOU FEEL DISAPPOINTED

When it comes to complex problems that involve both inside aspects (like thoughts and feelings) and outside factors (like other people, situations, and external experiences), my bias is to start with the inside then move to the outside.

In the case of disappointment, this means starting with your expectations. Were they realistic? Reasonable? Did the other person agree to them or share them, or are you placing expectations on them without their awareness or acknowledgment, then feeling disappointed because you didn't get your way?

Disappointment may be signaling to you that you need to adjust or let go of your expectations, that if you can be more flexible and open, you may not feel so let down.

On the other hand, sometimes your expectations are completely reasonable, even healthy—for example, you may feel disappointed because someone you trust lied to you. In that case, disappointment is an important call to action. Perhaps you need to have a crucial conversation, set a boundary, end a relationship, or communicate more clearly what you want or need.

WHEN YOU'RE THE SOURCE OF DISAPPOINTMENT

It's not a pleasant experience to let someone down or feel like a disappointment to others. But, again, there is a question of where the real problem is. Are they disappointed because you actually did something wrong or questionable? Did you agree to their expectations, then not uphold your end of the deal? Or did they place a demand on you without your consent or even awareness?

Keep in mind that someone else being disappointed in you may have more to do with their expectations than with anything you did or didn't do. In that case, it's important to recognize that their disappointment is *their* problem, not yours.

In contrast, sometimes their disappointment (or your disappointment in yourself) may be an absolutely natural reaction, and you can use that as a gut check moment. Are you behaving in a way that is consistent with your values? Are you being the kind of person you want to be? Do you need to work harder? Do things differently? You can use the pain of disappointment to motivate yourself to make changes and to grow as a person.

Then there are times when things get really complicated, when it's not an either/or situation, either it's your problem or theirs. Sometimes disappointment is both natural AND not a sign of a problem.

Have you ever really wanted to spend time with someone, like your best friend or your partner, but they had something important come up that got in the way? It would be completely understandable, completely human, to feel disappointed. You were looking forward to time together, but that reality is not coming to fruition. Yet, your expectation is not unreasonable, nor did they do anything wrong. You can be fully supportive of them doing the important thing that takes them away from you AND still experience disappointment. And they will need to work to understand that it's okay for you to feel disappointed AND that what they are doing is okay. That's a hard place to get to—it's advanced level emotional intelligence—but something to strive toward.

Navigating emotions like disappointment can be challenging, but understanding why we feel the way we do and learning what to do with that information can make all the difference.

"When you have expectations, you are setting yourself up for disappointment."

—RYAN REYNOLDS

MAKING SENSE OF THE SENSELESS: DEALING WITH TRAGEDY AND LOSS

Memorial Day in the U.S. is celebrated with three-day weekends, BBQs, and the opening of swimming pools. The true meaning of the holiday, however, is much more somber. It's a day dedicated to remembering those who died during military service, for honoring their sacrifice and that of their loved ones. For me, personally, it marks the anniversary of my brother's unexpected death many years ago. This year, in the wake of events centering on violence in schools and in my neighborhood, it feels particularly heavy, weighted by the unnecessary loss of life and those who must carry on with broken hearts. I find myself thinking about how we make sense out of tragedy, trauma, and loss.

How do we move forward in the face of unthinkable events?

I don't have the answers for addressing the systemic issues that lead to such horrific tragedies as war and school shootings. I don't even have all of the answers for how to cope with the fallout of these events or the loss of a loved one or the myriad other bad things that can leave scars on our lives. I do, however, have a knowledge base that sheds some insights, and I'm willing to share some of my own experiences on the off chance that it helps someone find hope in the darkness.

MAKING SENSE OUT OF THE SENSELESS

It's human nature to want the world to make sense. We like nice, neat explanations for events, and we want our cause-and-effect to be linear and straight forward. We like to think that good things happen to good people and that people who do bad things are evil. We like to think that it won't happen to us and that there is always a clear, easy-to-understand reason for why things happen. We like to think the world is just and logical. Unfortunately, it isn't.

When things happen that violate our idea of how the world works, our foundation gets shaken. We desperately need things to make sense again. In the aftermath of tragedy, our minds look for an explanation. They want to assign blame. If we can finger point to something that is clearly at fault, or better yet, if that someone or something is evil or greedy or broken or flawed, it restores our sense of balance. It rights the topsy-turviness that happened in our worlds. The issue is that it may not be that simple.

The assumptions we make about who is to blame may be faulty or myopic. They may not take into account all of the possible contributing factors. As tempting as it might be to put all of the blame on one person (or group) or one factor, my experience is that it's rarely that simple.

We need to understand what happened in a way that allows us to move forward. That likely means that we must expand our thinking and question our assumptions. We must sidestep faulty logic that leads to inaccurate or unhelpful conclusions. We must be intentional about meaning making because the story we tell ourselves about what happened, why it happened, and what it means about us, others, and the future will greatly shape our path.

IT'S NOT BLACK OR WHITE

There is a kind of therapy called Dialectical Behavior Therapy (DBT) that is based on the concept of dialectics, which are two opposing things that are both true. Dialectics are hard for our minds to navigate because they seem contradictory. Logic holds that if one is true then the other is not. Yet, they both are. The challenge is to simultaneously hold these contradictions and seek the broader truth, the one in which they both exist. We must resist the urge to throw one out in the interest of simplicity. We must resist the EITHER/OR and embrace the BOTH/AND mentality instead.

Today, I am embracing the dialectics. I find myself torn between seeing the world as utterly f-ed and seeing the incredible opportunities ahead, between being angered, disgusted, and devastated by the realities that our world is terrible and simultaneously awed and grateful for the wonder of that same reality.

Bad things happen to good people AND there is justice.

People are suffering AND there is beauty in the world.

We are on opposing sides AND we can collaborate.

I will never be the same AND I will find a way to have joy again.

FEEL YOUR FEELINGS

It's normal to feel a range of emotions following a foundation-shaking experience. We may feel sad, angry, guilty, anxious, confused, disgusted, and/or dozens of other ways. We may feel like we are going to be crushed by our pain or feel a strong urge to numb. As difficult as it may be, we must feel our feelings but not wallow in them. We must make space for them but not be buried by them. We will not be able to heal otherwise.

I remember walking in the hospital parking lot with my dad while my brother was on life support. "Do you want a Xanax?" he asked me.

"No," I told him. "This is supposed to hurt."

I'm not a masochist, but I *am* a psychologist. I had spent years at that point teaching people how important it is to experience rather than avoid even the most difficult, painful emotions. I am not judging my father for needing a Xanax in that moment. I have no idea the magnitude of a parent's pain in the face of losing a child. I'm not a parent myself. All I know is that I viewed my pain as important. It signaled to me how much I loved my brother and how much my world was being devastated. And in that moment, I had the capacity to hold my pain and weather the storm. In the moments since, I have continued to embrace the pain when it arises, to acknowledge that love and pain are two sides of the same coin, and to use that pain to fuel some of my actions and efforts.

In the face of personal or collective tragedy, it is important that we feel our emotions, that we heed their message, and that we consider what they are directing us to do. Perhaps, that means finding a way to honor our lost loved ones, finding a way to take meaningful action to affect real change, or finding the courage to experience joy again even with the heartache.

WISE MIND

One of the concepts I appreciate from DBT is called Wise Mind, which is the overlap of logic and emotion. When we operate from Wise Mind, we acknowledge and feel our feelings but are not ruled by them, and we listen to and are guided by logic but are not irrational, cold, or devoid of feeling. Finding this place of inner wisdom in the aftermath of tragedy or loss is important. Feel your feelings and take their message. Challenge your assumptions and faulty logic, but do let reason guide you. Take your next step with your head AND your heart.

THE CHOICE POINT

Victor Frankl, an Austrian psychiatrist and Holocaust survivor, wrote a famous book called *Man's Search for Meaning*. In it, he says, "Between every stimulus and response, there is a space. In that space is our power to choose our response. In our response lies our growth and our freedom."

Modern day psychologists often refer to this as the Choice Point. This is the fork in the road. We do not necessarily get to choose what happens to or around us, but we do get to choose what we do in the face of it. We get to choose who and how we want to be. We may not get to choose *what* we feel, but we can choose to feel it. We may not have the power to affect the change we want to see in our world, but we can decide to point fingers and play the blame game or we can take meaningful action. We can choose to go down the path of nihilistic despair or the one of growth and strength, if only we have the courage. We can channel our pain into a life that is worth living, even in a world that doesn't make sense.

"Between every stimulus and response, there is a space. In that space is our power to choose our response. In our response lies our growth and our freedom."

—VICTOR FRANKL

SHEDDING LIGHT ON SHAME

I didn't know if I was going to cry or vomit... or both. I was on the floor in the fetal position, near hysterics. I called my mom and told her what I'd done. She reassured me that it was the right thing.

I've technically been legally blind since I was a child. I have a blind spot in the center of my visual field, and it's always made fine details, like those letters on the eye chart, difficult to see. Over the years, the size of my blind spot expanded as did its impact on my functioning. Recognizing faces from any sort of distance became increasingly difficult as did reading print or screens. Still, I managed to find ways to minimize my flaw, relying on a good memory, context clues, excuses, and other sneaky compensatory strategies to mask the extent of my vision loss. It worked pretty well... until I had to stop driving. That change shoved me out of the disability closet, and that was a scary place to be.

My deteriorating retinas were forcing me to start the important work of coming to terms with my vision, and I was, admittedly, not doing a great job of it. I didn't realize it at the time, but it's because I was carrying around a vast amount of shame.

SHAME IS DARK

Shame is a beast of an emotion, although it doesn't always come roaring in the way anger or anxiety do. Instead, shame slips in quietly, working its way into the marrow of your bones. Shame is the voice that says *I am wrong. I am bad. I am unlovable and unworthy.* Shame is the feeling that says you are inherently flawed, that you are less than, unacceptable, damaged. It is a deep, dark fear of being shunned. *If others knew this about me, they would not, could not, accept me. Therefore, I must hide it.* And when we believe shame and follow its guidance to camouflage those aspects of ourselves or our histories, its hold gets stronger. It takes root and begins to grow. It is insidious, infiltrating the very core of our being until we don't even realize it's there. It is heavy and dark, and it likes it that way.

It is only in hindsight that I recognize the power that shame held over me for so many years. It is the reason I learned to fake sight so well (and avoided the situations where I couldn't). Shame prevented me from speaking up in class to say I couldn't read the board or being open with my friends. It made me burst into tears whenever my family mentioned my eyes. It kept me from asking for help and encouraged me to settle for things and people that weren't really that great for me. It subtly influenced me in hundreds of ways and silently directed thousands of my decisions. It convinced me that I was fundamentally not as good as other people and fueled self-doubt that lingered even after I built confidence in so many other areas. I didn't appreciate the psychological weight I was carrying around until it was gone.

BREAKING FREE FROM SHAME

As I had to confront the reality that I couldn't hide anymore, I begrudgingly began to have conversations about my limitations with my then partner, boss, colleagues, friends, and patients, solely on a need-to-know basis. Then, I blew things up that fetal position night.

I had decided to raise money for the Foundation Fighting Blindness, an organization that funds research into treatments for conditions like the one I have and, frankly, my best hope for a cure. As part of those efforts, I typed out my story, then published it to my public fundraising page, which I shared on social media and through email, ensuring that virtually everyone who knew me also now knew my shameful secret.

That's when I melted down. Coincidentally, that's also when things really began to shift for me.

By bringing into the open the very thing I had spent decades trying to hide, I had to face that deep, dark fear that I would be ostracized. Doing so gave me a chance to see that the fear was unfounded as no one actually treated me differently (or at least not different in a bad way). Interestingly, I also noticed that I felt a little lighter, at least once the hysteria, which was just shame throwing a temper tantrum, subsided. That was a turning point.

Now that my disability was common knowledge, I didn't have to work so hard to hide it, to pretend to be like everyone else. As I continued to be more open, I also began to become more matter of fact about it, eventually getting to the place where I am now, which is unashamed and truly accepting of my disability. Heck, I can even crack jokes (and write a book) about it these days!

I am not the only one who has had this experience. So many of my brave patients have shed light on their shame by sharing it with me or with others in their lives. As they opened up about their mental health diagnosis, the intrusive thoughts they thought were unique to them, the things they've done in the past that they were convinced made them a bad person, and the things that happened to them that made them feel like damaged goods, those facets began to matter less; the accompanying sense of shame was released.

As any child who is fearful at bedtime knows, things look scary in the dark. Convinced that there's a monster in their bedroom, when the lights turn on, they realize with relief that it was just a shadow. That thing about you, your body, your mind, your habits, your past, that thing that makes you less than, unworthy, bad… it's just a shadow. A shame shadow that will dissipate when it hits the light.

NOTES OF CAUTION

Do not be surprised if your first time sharing a shameful secret is terrifying. I know mine was, and I know that it got easier each subsequent time, as tends to be the case when it comes to confronting fears. I will also say that, at least in my experience, eradicating shame wasn't a one-time lightbulb moment but rather the result of a series of repeatedly being open about my visual impairment. It was a gradual process that was ignited that fateful fetal position night.

While I believe that sharing our secret shame is the way to let it go and to begin the process of healing from its damage, there are times when doing so may backfire. It is important to test the waters with a safe person, someone who cares about you, is empathetic, and isn't quick to criticize. If you muster your courage to talk with someone about your innermost vulnerabilities and they respond with judgment, shame will double down. It will rail against you. *I told you! You are bad. This proves it.* Do not be deterred, dear friend. Once is a fluke. Please be brave enough to try again.

And if you ever have the privilege of being the one to shed light on someone else's shame, honor their courage by responding with empathy and kindness. Put yourself in their shoes and understand what they've gone through or why they did what they did.

Embrace and accept them for who and what they are. Together, we can shine light into our dark nooks and crannies and diminish the power of shame.

"If you put shame in a petri dish, it needs three ingredients to grow exponentially: secrecy, silence, and judgment. If you put the same amount of shame in the petri dish and douse it with empathy, it can't survive."

—BRENE BROWN

BRIDGING THE DIVIDE THROUGH COURAGE, CURIOSITY, AND COMPASSION

I am not known for my sense of fashion. I never have been, but it's admittedly gotten worse the past few years as I've worked from home and embraced comfort. Some friends tease me about my "party cardy"—I am definitely a fan of the cardigan—while my blunter friends are a little more direct: "Doc, try harder. You're not dead yet."

Sometimes tough love is needed.

In an effort to spruce up the wardrobe last summer, I begrudgingly bought a few crop tops. Can a 40-some-odd-year-old woman get away with wearing a crop top? Apparently, the answer these days is yes. But perhaps the question is *should* she? I couldn't help but think, *is this a bit of a mid-life crisis moment, trying to cling to youth? Am I too old for this?*

I'M TOO OLD FOR THIS

I generally despise the phrase, "I'm too old for/to..." because I don't agree with those limits. I intend to be mobile and active, playful and adventurous well into senior citizenhood. That said, I do hope to carry wisdom forward with youthful wonder and leave harmful, juvenile antics behind.

I wish America would do the same.

On July 4, 2024, the United States will turn 248. Yet, she's been acting like an angsty, ungrateful teen lately. It's not a good look.

AMERICA'S MID-LIFE CRISIS

My first job out of grad school was at Omaha Children's Hospital. I provided outpatient therapy for a ton of teenagers. They were dramatic and oh so entertaining. I got a kick out of watching how their developing minds worked. They'd get caught up in these big feelings—so angry—and would spout their justifications out. If I or their parents responded in a calm logical manner to whatever concern or complaint they voiced, did they accept that and move forward? Nope. Their minds would snake a different direction, finding a new argument to justify their feelings. It was like they just wanted to be mad. Logic was lost on them.

I remember reading a book with a catchy title along the lines of *Yes, Your Teen Is Crazy* in which the author compared adolescents to brain-damaged individuals, given the rate at which their brains were developing and changing. He described them as moody and irrational. It was so insightful and so spot on.

And I think America is acting like a giant teenager when she's old enough to know better.

It's one thing to wear a crop top and quite another to wild out in ways that do real damage.

We're a big country here in the U.S. with tons of people representing tons of lifestyles, belief systems, and viewpoints. It's a beautiful thing. At least it can be. Except that we seem to be getting increasingly polarized, angry, and individualistic. We have big feelings, and we're not handling them well.

LAND OF THE FREE AND HOME OF THE BRAVE

There is perhaps no ideal more central to being American than freedom. We expect it. We demand it. And we fight for it. But have you noticed that, lately, we seem to be fighting *against* it?

When I think about freedoms and America, there is this base assumption that as a capable adult, I should be able to make my own decisions, to live my life in accordance with my values, as long as I pay my taxes and don't do anything to interfere with someone else living their life.

You do you, as long as you doing you doesn't stop me from doing me.

Yet, somehow, here we are. People are clinging desperately to their particular brand of freedom and, in doing so, are imposing it on others, thus taking away theirs. It's quite the conundrum. How did we get here?

That's a complicated question with a complicated answer, I'm sure. What I'm also sure about is that we've gotten increasingly judgmental. We're quick to pass judgment that others are wrong, bad, or shouldn't be that way. We've forgotten how to be tolerant, generous, and kind.

STOP BEING SO JUDGMENTAL

To really embrace freedom, I think we need to step outside of our judgments. And they *are* judgments. We may treat them as fact, committed to the notion that our perspective is the right one, mistaking it as fact when it is really belief. Instead of being so righteous in our judgments masquerading as facts, we need to embrace each other with curiosity.

Please note, I'm not taking political sides here. I'm calling everyone on all sides out and asking us all to do a little better, to remember the things we learned in kindergarten about getting along—share, take turns, don't call names, be kind.

To be curious, not judgmental.

And it takes courage to be curious. It takes courage to consider that our beliefs are cognitive constructs, things our minds created, rather than some objective truth. It takes courage to be willing to consider that there may be other ways or other perspectives. It takes courage to set fear and the hate that often hides it aside, and it takes courage to connect with others, especially when they seem different.

Fortunately, America is the home of the brave... if only we can remember what it actually means to be brave.

In my psychology practice, I specialize in treating anxiety disorders, which more or less boils down to helping people learn how to feel afraid and still do what matters, how to keep fear from making their decisions, in essence, how to be brave. It's not just my patients, though, who need to work on this. I can't help but wonder, what would happen if everyone got a little braver? What if we approached each other and each divisive issue from a perspective of curiosity and courage? Moreover, what would happen if we threw in a little compassion as well?

THE ANTIDOTE TO ANGER

Several years ago, I visited Ireland. As their version of a TSA agent checked my bag at the airport, he was all smiles, eye contact, and conversation. It was a lovely small talk experience, one human being to another. Then, I landed at O'Hare in Chicago and was immediately struck by the anger. TSA agents were yelling at travelers. Travelers were yelling at each other. It was such a stark contrast, and it felt like a punch in the gut. Americans are angry... in general.

This wasn't during a particularly charged time in history. It was a couple years pre-COVID and everything else that's transpired since. Still, the hostility and animosity were rampant, and it made me sad for us.

Anger has its place and purpose in our existence. It's better as the exception than the rule, though, if you are at all concerned with living a happy life. The more time we spend in an angry state, the poorer our psychological wellbeing.

Increasingly, anger seems coupled with hate, and those two emotions are powerful... and destructive. Wise teachers like the Buddha, Thich Nhat Hanh, and the Dalai Lama, who offer sage advice on how to reduce human suffering and find inner peace regardless of your religious beliefs, all hold that compassion is the antidote to anger and hate.

Compassion is a skill, and one that we all need a crash course in. How much better would everything be if we could tap into compassion, along with that curiosity and courage?

If we dig far enough below all of the identity politics and hot button topics, beneath the anger and fear, we all want the same things. We want to be happy, healthy, safe, and secure.

These are not zero sum games. There is plenty of happiness to go around. My health does not detract from yours, nor does my safety or security.

It's time to stop fighting for the sake of fighting, to stop getting caught up in the unnecessary drama, and to stop blaming others. It's time to focus less on being right or winning, and it's time to focus on being good humans.

"Fight for the things you care about, but do it in a way that will lead others to join you."

—RUTH BADER GINSBURG

SECTION 3

Navigating Relationships

Few things in life matter as much as the people in it. In fact, having quality relationships is one of, if not the biggest contributor to our overall life satisfaction. Who we surround ourselves with and give our precious time to dictates so much.

Our relationships influence who we become, the decisions we make, and the way we live our lives. They can give us a sense of purpose, a lifeline when we're drowning, a secure foundation from which to venture out, and a safety net to catch us when we fall. They can amplify our successes and our joys. They can bring out the best in us and in life.

They can also bring out the worst.

Bad ones can leave us feeling like a shell of ourselves, isolated, and lonely. They can drag us down and dampen our spirit. They can cause so much strife, insecurity, and even outright harm.

Navigating other people can be complicated. Forging healthy, strong bonds requires certain skills, which, fortunately, can be honed over time. We can learn how to smooth over friction, handle conflict, communicate effectively, and build intimacy and trust. Ultimately, I believe that relationships are living, breathing things. They are constantly evolving, as are the people involved in them. They necessitate—and deserve—work, so let's get to it.

GROWING, THRIVING, OR DYING? A QUESTION OF SOCIAL SOIL

I used to live in a downtown apartment with two windows that I rarely opened because I don't see well in sunlight. I have an aloe plant, a poor yet hardy thing that somehow survived a year in those conditions. Apparently, I gave it just enough water and the occasional open blind to keep it alive, but it was definitely not thriving.

The same thing can happen to us.

Many wise people have said something to the effect of: "In this life, you are either growing or dying." I agree. That process of wilting and dying, though, can sometimes be slow, sneaky, going undetected for long periods of time. And whether we thrive or wilt depends heavily on our social soil.

Let's assume that, genetically speaking, you're a rose, and I'm a lily. You will always be a rose, and I will always be a lily. No matter how hard you or I try to be something different, it's just not going to happen. The soil that we are in, however, will have a huge impact on how our lily-ness and rose-ness are expressed.

If I'm in fertile, nourishing soil, I'm going to grow into a luscious, vibrant lily. I will reach my full blooming potential. If I'm in toxic soil, however, I'm going to end up a shriveled brown version of that.

As people, our social soil—the relationships and social systems we find ourselves in—matter. They shape us, either supporting us, allowing and encouraging us to become the fullest, most vibrant versions of ourselves, or they limit our growth, even causing damage, in some way.

Our social soil includes our two-way relationships like romantic partners, friends, parent/child, as well as the bigger and more complicated social contexts in which we exist like families, workplaces, and various communities. We find ourselves in these environments both intentionally, the result of active choices, and passively, through unintentional choice or happenstance.

Sometimes, when the soil is super toxic, it's hard to miss. You can tell immediately—this doesn't look right, smell right, feel right. This is not good for me! Other times, though, it can actually be pretty difficult to recognize toxic soil. You wake up one day, look back, and realize that you have slowly been withering away as a person.

Perhaps the hardest is when originally fertile soil turns toxic. There have been some times in my life when I found myself planted in what seemed to be healthy soil. I was excited, growing, prospering… then gradually the dynamics shifted. Over time, the result was halted growth. I found myself wilting, becoming a less vital version of me. That's a hard reality to accept, especially when you have invested a lot of time and energy into that particular soil.

Another hard reality to accept is that *you* may be toxic soil for someone else. As much as I hate to admit it, I am quite sure that there have been times when I inadvertently stunted the growth of my loved ones or others around me. Instead of bringing out the best in them, I heaped on to them, weighing them down.

I am not a bad person, and those people and places who were toxic for me are not necessarily bad, either. Sure, some may be, but it seems more gracious to assume otherwise. How, then, can they be toxic? To mix metaphors here, sometimes two people come together like baking soda and vinegar. On their own, they are fine, useful, perfectly stable. Together... boom! Volcanic reaction.

Obvious conclusion? Get out of toxic soil if at all possible, even if it's scary or difficult to muster the energy to change. It's also time to get real with yourself. Are you lifting others up? Helping them grow? Pay attention to the impact that your soils are having on you. Ask yourself, am I thriving or wilting?

"Personal relationships are the fertile soil from which all advancement, all success, all achievement in real life grows."

—BEN STEIN

TAKING OFF THE MASK: LETTING YOUR AUTHENTIC SELF BE SEEN

While you may think that Halloween is the only time we wear masks, I bet a good number of us wear masks a good chunk of the time. We hide our insecurities with bravado. Our flaws masquerade behind perfectionism. Our need to belong is shielded by agreeableness. We pretend like we're fine when we're not, that we're happy with things that bother us, that we're in control, that we've got it all together. We mold ourselves to meet others' perceived expectations, not always realizing the toll that doing so takes on us.

I read a quote this week that was a bit of a gut punch, but it summed things up beautifully: "I think the reward for conformity is that everyone likes you except yourself."

Let that sink in.

WHY DO WE DO IT?

As important as healthy relationships are to our quality of life—even our longevity—forming tight bonds isn't always easy. We all want to be understood, accepted, and valued for who we are, not just what we can do or provide for others. Yet, opening ourselves up to intimate scrutiny can be incredibly uncomfortable. When we think about taking off the mask, of letting our authentic selves out for the world to see, we feel vulnerable.

And you know what? Vulnerability sucks!

That feeling that comes when we're exposed and unsure of the outcome, of how others are going to respond to us or what will happen, leaves us with an icky, small, even shameful, emotional residue. *That* feeling is vulnerability.

In those moments, our soft underbellies are exposed, and we're open to the possibility of getting hurt. What if we're honest with someone and they have a negative reaction? What if we let people see our flaws and they reject us? What if there are repercussions for our honesty and the blowback isn't good? What if we express what we really need and we end up disappointed?

A lot of times, those possibilities just seem too risky, so we mask up. Nod and smile. Stay silent. Hem and haw. Beat around the bush. Act like you don't care. Lash out. Lie. Deceive. Pretend. Fake it. Minimize. Play small. Invalidate.

With the protection of our masks, we jump back into our comfort zones, relieved that we are no longer fully on display. Yet, doubt takes hold. When we hide our true selves from others, the little voice in the back of our minds lingers. It whispers things like: *Sure, everyone likes you, but it's a facade. They don't know the real you. You have their respect now, but you'd lose it if... They'll judge you if they know... Bad things will happen if you let any of this show.*

And so we mask to stay safe and to fit in, but it's not the same as belonging.

BUT... VULNERABILITY IS BRAVE

Real intimacy, truly being known, requires the courage to be open about who you really are, what you really think and feel, and what you really want and need.

I can't tell you how many people are moving through life right now feeling lonely, desperately longing for connection... while desperately clinging to their masks. The idea of expressing themselves wholly and honestly, even to their partners, best friends, or long-time colleagues, seems entirely too risky.

When we guard ourselves, we build a wall to keep us safe. But walls also keep others out. It's a catch-22.

To feel a level of connection, *real* connection, we must be willing to take a risk, to be vulnerable. So, while vulnerability sucks, it is also one of the bravest things possible.

BEING REAL IS WORTH THE RISK

With courage and a willingness to be uncomfortable, I am learning just how valuable vulnerability is. For me, some of the most potent lessons came shortly after I stopped driving.

Up until that point, I was pretty quiet about my visual impairment. Driven by shame and a deeply convincing belief that I would be shunned in all possible ways if others knew, I got really good at faking sight. Unfortunately, there's no real way to do that when it comes to driving a motor vehicle. So, I had to take that mask off.

The first time I shared publicly about my disability was one of the scariest moments for me. But it turned out well, and I got to see that people weren't nearly as horrified as I'd envisioned they'd be.

Fast forward a bit. My vision was becoming common knowledge but asking for help wasn't. Hiding and masking were still my defaults. Then, I found myself at the studio where I used to practice swing dancing with a pretty big group, some of whom I'd known for years and some I didn't actually know at all. We were getting ready for a competition weekend. I was newly single and facing the prospect of walking into a large ballroom on my own.

At the time, that was one of the most intimidating things for me. Walking into a large room by myself and trying to find my people is hard. Because of the nature of my vision, I have trouble seeing faces clearly from any distance, so that leaves me wandering aimlessly, looking (*feeling*) like an idiot. It's daunting.

So, I decided to be brave and announce to the entire practice group that doing that was difficult, and I asked if they could please wave or, even better, come over and get me if they saw me walk in. Of course, everyone was supportive. I got hugs and texts and offers for rides. It was overwhelming. *Not all in a good way.*

When I got home, I sobbed. Like ugly cry sobbing.

It wasn't a feeling of appreciation or support or love. It was, what I have since learned is called, a vulnerability hangover. The recoil that comes from putting yourself out there so unprotected.

It wasn't pleasant. But it was powerful.

On the other side of that experience came closeness. Some friends who had known me for years now knew me differently, and we both felt closer for it.

On the other side of that experience also came confidence. My ability to accept my vision and trust in myself both grew.

I learned important lessons that day: 1) That the little voice that says others will reject you isn't always right and 2) That I can do hard things. Those lessons, which have served me well in so many ways over the years, were hard-won and absolutely would not have been possible without vulnerability.

The experience got me thinking about how I can continue to take off my remaining metaphorical masks. I now ask myself, where am I being truly authentic and what am I shying away from? How might I let my guard down?

Do you have the courage to join me?

"I think the reward for conformity is that everyone likes you except yourself."

—RITA MAE BROWN

THE SOCIAL EXPERIMENT TO FEEL MORE CONNECTED

My phone rang. *Why is Mackie calling?* I thought. He's one of my brunch friends. We usually catch up over biscuits or beignets. Sometimes we exchange sassy comments in our group chat. Occasionally, we grab coffee, text, or hop on a phone call when there's something specific to talk about. But he'd never called me completely out of the blue before.

"You were on my mind," he said by way of greeting. He explained that when he finds himself thinking of someone, he takes it as a sign that he needs to reach out. We chatted for a few minutes about nothing in particular before going on about our days, mine now feeling a little brighter.

Around the same time, maybe a few weeks before or a few after, my little brother, who dispenses sage advice surprisingly often, said the same thing—when he thinks of someone, he shoots them a text just to let them know.

As different as they are, Joe and Mackie are both people who have people, wide networks and real friendships. And they both echoed the importance of nurturing relationships and how seizing the moment to connect is an easy and effective way for them to do that.

I was inspired.

LONELINESS IS AN EPIDEMIC

I used that phrase years before the Surgeon General, whose 2023 report called out the need to heal loneliness and social isolation. The reality is that the rates of loneliness (in the U.S. at least) have been increasing for decades, with 1 in 2 adults experiencing it... and that was *before* COVID.

Humans are inherently social creatures, wired for kinship, and loneliness isn't just an uncomfortable thing. It's actually quite harmful, raising the risk for mental health issues and impacting our physical health as well. (Loneliness is on par with smoking in terms of impact on mortality, and it outpaces obesity and a sedentary lifestyle. Yikes.) Clearly, we need to figure out a remedy.

THE SOCIAL EXPERIMENT

During various stages throughout my life, I have felt disconnected, if not downright lonely. I have often envied people like Mackie who seem to know everyone and to always have a full social calendar because I have often longed to feel that deeply connected.

A theme of the present phase of my life has been to make that happen. I have been seeking out and fostering relationships, both personal and professional. Through countless networking coffee meetups, hours-long catch-up calls with old friends, and being more open and vulnerable with people generally, I've made notable progress in that area.

I still didn't feel as rooted in relationships as I would like though, so I decided to take a page out of their book. Joe and Mackie both find the you-popped-in-my-head-so-I'm-reaching-out-approach to be helpful, but would it work for me?

Once is a fluke. Twice is a coincidence. But three times is a pattern. I've been running their experiment for a few months now... and I think they're onto something. I feel more at ease and connected than I have in a really long time. I've noticed a few other interesting things, too.

INTERESTING FINDINGS

Changing up habits—and that's what this experiment really is, a change in relationship habits, implementing new rhythms and rituals of connection—isn't the easiest thing to do. What *is* easy is to come up with excuses not to do it, to not reach out. Excuses like: *I'll call them later. They might be busy. They're probably working right now. I don't have time to get into a big, long conversation. I don't want to overstep. It's been so long. I don't even know where to start. Or it's been so long, it'll be weird to reach out now. Or it's been so long, they're probably upset with me.* Whatever it is, it kind of boils down to two main concerns: I don't have time and they'll have a negative reaction.

Those excuses may seem valid, but they're really just an attempt to justify avoiding something that is either a little uncomfortable or a little different than your usual m.o. Either way, I've found that if you simply ignore the excuses and send the text or email anyways, they tend to quiet down, but let's get into the weeds here.

I Don't Have Time

You do. You actually do. Even just a few minutes that show you're invested in the relationship make a difference. You can preface a conversation with, "I only have a few minutes, but I wanted to hear about XYZ." With just a little willingness to be direct, you can connect in a meaningful way without it taking a ton of time. You're not actually obligated to have a deep or lengthy conversation.

Similarly, I've found that shooting a quick message to share something interesting, ask about something going on in their life, or just to say thinking of you hasn't resulted in me being chained to my phone in a marathon text exchange. It's okay to set the phone aside and go on about your business, just like Joe advised. No time lost; connection gained.

They'll Have a Negative Reaction

As for the excuses and fears that the person on the receiving end might be bothered in some way, I just haven't had that experience. I suppose it's possible that they're responding favorably while harboring all kinds of judgments about me, but I just choose not to believe that. I know that when I've been fortunate enough to be the reach out*ee* instead of the reach out*er*, I've been flattered or felt cared for. That little bit of extra effort feels so nice, so real. In a world where we're constantly connected, yet disconnected, from ourselves and others in deep meaningful ways, this matters.

WHERE DO WE GO FROM HERE?

Relationships are like plants. They must be watered and tended in order to grow and blossom. And when they are neglected, they wither and die. In an age of loneliness, cultivating relationships is especially important. How might you nurture yours a bit more today?

"We've got this gift of love, but love is like a precious plant. You can't just accept it and leave it in the cupboard or just think it's going to get on by itself. You've got to keep watering it. You've got to really look after it and nurture it."

—JOHN LENNON

BEYOND THE SURFACE: TAPPING INTO EMPATHY AND ASSUMING POSITIVE INTENT

I am many things, but stupid is not one of them. Yet, I've been treated as though I am on more than one occasion, typically by airline staff.

There was the woman who stared at me incredulously and pointed to the little indicator on the bathroom door when I asked if the restroom was occupied.

There was the other woman who repeatedly asked me for my flight number, refusing to look at the boarding pass I held out to her. She finally relented when I said, "Hold on. I'll have to get out my magnifier. I'm visually impaired and can't see the small print. That's why I was trying to show it to you."

My vision impairment makes it difficult for me to do some things that involve seeing fine details like whether the little slot on the bathroom door is red or green or the screens that post flight gates. So, I have to ask for help.

The issue, though, is that because of the nature of my particular vision loss, I don't have any outward indicator that I'm disabled. I don't need a white cane or a guide dog. I don't typically wear sunglasses inside. There's nothing to mark me as different to strangers, so when I'm asking for help for something that seems routine or obvious, their assumption is that I must be stupid or unobservant.

It's not my favorite experience, but I get it.

HOW OUR MINDS MISGUIDE US

You can't judge a book by its cover, but we all do because we are human and that's how our brains work. I understand, more than most thanks to my profession and my deep passion for all things brain science, that our minds take shortcuts when it comes to processing information. They quickly take in all the details of a situation, discard a ton of the data on the basis that it is irrelevant, then resort to further shortcuts, biases, and heuristics (rules of thumb) to make meaning and provide guidance on what to do.

It's a lot.

And they consistently, predictably, cause errors in the way we think.

One of the most fundamental of those built-in biases is the negativity bias, which refers to our mind's natural tendency to notice and hold on to bad stuff. Essentially, unless intentionally trained to do otherwise, our mind's default is to go negative.

Then there's the fundamental attribution error in which our minds explain the behaviors of others based on character rather than circumstances. The fundamental attribution error is what causes you to yell at that other driver who is an inconsiderate jerk when cutting you off while cutting yourself some slack when you do the same thing. You obviously made an honest mistake while the other guy is deplorable.

Let's not forget the judgment shortcut, either. Judgments are a quick categorization of *good* or *bad*, or *I like this* or *I don't like this*. They save a lot of time. Compare *that's bad* to *someone is looking at me with a furrowed brow and downturned mouth. They are breathing heavily. Their shoulders are shrugged up indicating muscle tension. They must be angry. At me. This isn't going to go well.* The judgment cuts to the chase so much faster... but judgments can lead to anxiety, sadness, anger, guilt, or some other emotion that isn't necessarily warranted.

Finally, our minds tend to make things all about us. It's not that we're self-centered intentionally. It's just that our minds automatically jump to me—how does this affect me and my survival? For example, when you felt anxious about that person not texting you back, it was because they might be blowing you off, right? Not because they might've dropped their phone in the toilet or forgot to bring a charger with them.

This last one has caused me some strife for sure. Like the time in high school when my friend's mom called to inform mine just how disrespectful and rude her daughter was... because I didn't wave to her from across the parking lot. Or the patient who worked so hard and made so much progress in therapy who thought I was disappointed or upset with her when I didn't say hi. (It still makes me sad to know I inadvertently caused her pain.) They didn't know about my vision.

TAPPING INTO EMPATHY

It is up to each of us to learn about our brain's built-in biases and how they may be wreaking havoc on our experiences and our relationships. When we do this, we are poised to be more empathetic and, frankly, better friends, family members, colleagues, and humans.

But what if we took it farther and assumed positive intent? Then, when someone did or said something that was "bad," perhaps we could consider: *People are basically good. They just did something that isn't, according to my mind. What's the kindest explanation for their behavior?* Rather than assuming the worst or assassinating their character or going negative or making it all about us, maybe we'd pause to consider, perhaps, that driver isn't an idiot who got their license out of a Cracker Jack box. Maybe, they're a great driver who's in a hurry because they're about to get sick. How would that point of view play out? We'd be calmer, kinder, and less likely to react with aggression. That's so much better than fuming and honking and carrying that stress with us, right?

And maybe our assuming positive intent means recognizing that we're all human, and we all get caught up in our default habitual thinking patterns, and maybe we can find patience and compassion rather than responding in kind.

"When working with people, assume good intentions. When listening to people, interpret their words in a generous way. You will occasionally get burned and mistreated by always assuming the best in others, but it is a far better way to live than the opposite."

—JAMES CLEAR

THE BLAME GAME

I t's a rigged game, much like that carnival one in which you throw ping-pong balls into goldfish bowls. Sure, if you're spectacularly lucky, you might launch the ball at just the right angle with the precise amount of rotation, taking into account the wind speed and direction and the moon's gravitational pull. The odds of taking home a fish are definitely stacked against you. They're stacked against you in the Blame Game, too.

Here are the rules of the game:

1. A problem happens, anything from a minor someone forgetting to do a household chore to a major national tragedy.

2. Players must quickly point out the problem, point their finger at someone else, and argue why it's the other player's fault.

3. Adamantly defend your position.

4. The blame is volleyed back and forth until someone wins.

Just kidding. No one wins. Why?

As soon as we start blaming, it becomes a You v. Me rather than a We situation. The debate becomes about being right and defending your ego, and giving an inch toward compromise feels like a loss. When was the last time you told someone what she did was wrong or accused him of messing up, and you got the response, "Gee, you're right. Thanks for letting me know. I'll do whatever you think is best to fix it"?

Yeah, I didn't think so.

When we play the Blame Game, we're too busy passing the buck or protecting our ego (it hurts to be wrong, am I right?) to focus on a solution. Moreover, hurtful things are said, and hurtful feelings on both sides grow.

AND NO ONE WINS.

In fact, I'd argue you're actually even *less* likely to have your point of view heard and accepted during the Blame Game. Sure, maybe someone gets the last word. Maybe it's even you. When the silence falls, though, take a moment to survey the damage. Still feel like a winner? You get to be right, but did it fix the problem? Is your relationship better off than it was? Was it worth it?

I learned the hard way that in relationships, sometimes the choice is: Do I want to be right, or do I want to be happy?

"You said you'd take out the trash!"

"No, I didn't."

"Yes, you did. I remember it because blah, blah, blah."

"No, I did NOT say that. You must've misheard." Etc.

What we have here, folks, is an impasse. There's no way to know objectively who is right. Even if there were, would it really matter? Continuing to defend your rightness won't take out the trash. Besides, by the end of it, I'd venture to guess that neither of you is very happy.

Wouldn't it make more sense to take a second to ask yourself, "What's really important here?" A) being right, B) making the other person feel like crap, or C) figuring out how to get the damn trash out of the house so we can move on.

C. The answer is always C.

This advice applies to relationships between individuals (friends, partners, parents/children, coworkers, boss/employee) as well as groups. (Hello, current bipartisan political system.) The Blame Game, as appealing as it might be, doesn't end well for anyone.

In many instances, blame is useless at best and can often be quite harmful. Everyone is going to be better off if we each take responsibility for our own contributions to the problem and let others claim their own piece of the responsibility pie. Whether they do or not, spend your time and energy focusing on a solution. The problem gets addressed, lots of hurts get avoided, and we can move on.

"If you point a finger at someone, there are three fingers pointing back at you."

—SOURCE UNKNOWN

WHAT DO YOU MEAN BY THAT? HOW SPECIFICITY CREATES CLARITY

They weren't trying to annoy me, but they were doing a fantastic job.

I was at a Village Inn with my two closest grad school friends, talking about my thesis proposal. I was studying the links between happiness, optimism, and social anxiety in teenagers. After I walked them through my research plans, they asked the most annoying question ever... "What do you mean by happiness?"

"You know, happiness," I spurted.

"Yes, but how are you defining happiness?" they pressed. In order to measure something, they pointed out, you have to know exactly what it is.

They were right, of course, but it was a really frustrating moment because I just didn't know how to answer the question. Happiness is something we all know, right? Or do we conflate pleasure, enjoyment, contentment, the absence of pain, satisfaction, and a myriad of other positive emotional experiences? We lump a number of different things into this one term "happiness" as though they are interchangeable. Is it any wonder that it can be so elusive?

THE IMPORTANCE OF PRECISION

In science, we must operationally define the things we study. That's what my friends were trying to help me do. The task is to be so concrete and precise that another researcher could study the exact same thing with no room for interpretation or confusion. It's not just research where precision matters, though. Individually, making decisions toward long-term goals gets easier the more specific and defined those goals are. Interpersonally, precision helps strengthen relationships and avoid friction.

With Ourselves

This point was really illuminated for me by my dear friend and Peak Mind co-founder, April. We were chatting about the awesome Disney World adventure she orchestrated for her daughters. While I'm thrilled she had a fabulous family vacation, the part that was *really* exciting to me was her behind-the-scenes thought process.

Like most parents, April wanted her girls to have a great time at Disney. That sounds like a clear, specific goal... but it's as vague as "happiness."

April shared how she really dug down on that goal to get clear about what she was truly after. To her, she knew that "great time" meant a powerful core memory based on an experience full of positive emotions and wonder. That precision gave her direction on how to design the day. Rather than waking up extra early to get the most *time* at Disney, she opted to let her girls sleep in knowing that being well-rested would lead to better moods and more joy than being overly tired and cranky. The outcome? A beautiful day that her whole family loved.

A lightbulb went off. I left our conversation rethinking my own goals. I have felt a strong sense of clarity around what I want to accomplish in several domains, from business to health to relationships, yet I sometimes find myself struggling to know what to do next. I realized that if I spend some time drilling down, getting even more precise about what it is I'm after, I will have a simpler, clearer path to follow. That insight was actionable and energizing.

With Others

It wasn't just my talk with April that highlighted the importance of precision. The same theme has come up in several ways with regard to boundaries and relationships.

Set clear boundaries. Great advice... but what *are* those boundaries? Specifically. What are you willing and not willing to do? Where are your lines? If you aren't crystal clear on them, how can you communicate them to and enforce them with other people?

Speaking of other people, so many miscommunications and misunderstandings happen when we think we're being really clear. While we may be using the same language, what we *mean* (or think the other person means) may be very different.

I need support might be quite clear to you... and to your loved one... but your definitions of support might vary tremendously. Perhaps yours means taking tasks off your plate while theirs means giving you a hug and encouraging words.

WHAT DO YOU MEAN BY THAT?

When you take the time to wade through the annoyance that might initially arise, clarifying exactly what you mean will prove beneficial for you as you make decisions and navigate how you spend your resources, likely helping you achieve what you truly want faster.

Pausing to ask, "What do you mean by that?" to another person can help ensure that you're on the same page and that no one is operating on misguided assumptions. Just imagine how much turmoil could've been avoided if Ross and Rachel had been explicit about what it means to be on a break? (That's a *Friends* reference for the youngsters out there.)

The takeaway point here is that even when you *think* you're being clear about what you want or what you're after, you need to get really granular by asking, "What do you mean by that?" And keep asking until you get to the most specific, clear place you can. Then run with that.

"Clarity is power. The more clear you are about what you want the more likely you are to achieve it."

—BILLY COX

VALIDATION: THE SKILL THAT WILL IMPROVE YOUR RELATIONSHIPS

"You don't understand me!"

"I *do* understand you. I just don't agree with you."

Dramatically rolling her eyes through tears, she looks at me. "She just doesn't get it. It's like she doesn't even care." The teen doesn't see the pained look of defeat on her mother's face.

That's me paraphrasing every therapy session with a 14-year-old and their parent ever.

Perhaps I'm the one being a tad dramatic here—it's not *every* single session... but I want to highlight what's really underneath the conflict and what's really doing relationship damage: a lack of validation.

From the bedroom to the boardroom and everywhere in between, successful, healthy relationships matter... and they don't happen by accident. Whether we're talking about personal or professional contexts, there are some key interpersonal skills that, as renowned experts the Drs. Gottman put it, separate the relationship masters from the disasters. Validation is one of them.

WHAT IS VALIDATION?

We know that relationships are important. Whether we're talking about quality of life on a personal level or being wildly successful in a professional capacity, it all boils down to relationships. Being able to build and maintain strong, healthy connections is critical.

As humans, we have a deep need to feel seen, heard, understood, appreciated, and accepted (even those of us who hate vulnerability or don't want to admit that we have those basic social human needs). And your ability to make *others* feel seen, heard, understood, appreciated, and accepted is a skill called validation. While some people seem to acquire validation skills intuitively, (most) others have to be trained, at least to some degree.

HOW TO VALIDATE OTHERS

Returning to our angsty teen and defeated mom, there are two points I want to call out here: empty words and conflating understanding and agreement.

Show, Don't Tell

Mom says the words, "I understand." She is *literally* telling her daughter that she gets it, yet her daughter doesn't feel understood. What gives?

While Mom is *trying* to validate her daughter, her efforts are falling flat. It's like the keto cookies my friend Brandon tried to pass off as dessert when I asked for an after-dinner sweet treat. Technically, it was a cookie, but without sugar and flour, it was a poor proxy. Chocolate cardboard was just no substitute for the real thing. I'd rather just not have any dessert at all.

When it comes to understanding others, show, don't tell. The trick is to demonstrate that you truly get it. Convince them that you absolutely know what they are feeling and why.

Here's what Mom meant to say. "I get it. Spending time with your friends is really important. I said no, and you don't think I have a good reason for that. It feels unfair and controlling, and that's super frustrating." How do you think that would've been received by her daughter?

When you validate someone else, you are acknowledging how they feel, showing that you get it, and, if you want to level it up a notch, assuring them that what they are feeling makes sense considering all of the contributing factors (like their personal history and the current circumstances). Here are some more examples of validating statements:

* "I can see how upset you are by this."

* "I understand that you're feeling overwhelmed. You've been under a tight deadline, and we're short-staffed."

* "Wow! Your coworker/friend/family member/neighbor sounds really arrogant. That must be so annoying!"

* And my personal favorite, the "of course!" "Of course you're feeling judged! Who wouldn't given those circumstances!"

* "Of course you're struggling! This is hard stuff. ANYONE would find this tough!"

Validating does not mean that you share their feelings or that you agree with the conclusions or decisions their feelings are leading them to, only that you can see how and why they are experiencing those feelings.

Which brings us to...

UNDERSTANDING IS NOT THE SAME AS AGREEMENT

Teens aren't the only ones who conflate understanding with agreement. I've seen many adults, in all manner of contexts, do the same thing. Heck, between you and me, I'm sure that we've both done it a time or two ourselves.

It's so easy to smoosh understanding and agreement together in our minds because we see ourselves as logical, rational beings. (We're not, but that's a soapbox for another day.) We assume that if someone else disagrees with us, it must be because they don't actually understand us. If they did, if they understood our (presumably trustworthy, accurate, and completely logical) thoughts and feelings, they would absolutely, 100% be on the same page. How could they not be?

It's because understanding and agreement are NOT the same thing. You can absolutely understand someone and still disagree with them.

Where relationships start to break down and conflict ensues is when validation is missing. Remember, you have to *show* that you understand—validate. Using this powerful skill prevents interactions from devolving, preserves bonds despite disagreements, and, if you really want to get effective, sets the stage for persuasion. People are much more likely to concede or compromise or even just accept undesired outcomes when they feel like they were *first* listened to and *actually* heard. Can you see how learning to validate others is worth your time?

SUPPORTING SOMEONE WITHOUT ACCIDENTAL INVALIDATION

Validation isn't just for conflict. It's also a useful skill when you want to provide support or deepen a connection.

Often, when someone we care about is struggling in some way (especially when it's completely unrelated to us so our own egos and emotions aren't getting in the way), we have a strong urge to help them feel better. Unfortunately, our efforts can backfire when they are inadvertently invalidating.

* "Don't feel sad/mad/bad."

* "Don't be upset."

* "You're okay" (when they clearly are not).

* "It's not that big of a deal."

* "This won't even matter in a week."

While the sentiment behind these statements—I don't want you to hurt—isn't wrong or bad, the unspoken message that gets conveyed is that their lived experience or reaction *is*. By trying to soften their pain, you may be amplifying it. Ouch.

You may eventually end up in the same place, offering the same condolences, perspectives, or advice, but start with validation if you want to strengthen the relationship or actually be supportive. Reflect back what they're feeling at a minimum. Just a single statement that acknowledges, rather than denies, reality at the moment can go a long way.

* "That's scary."

* "That's infuriating."

* "That's demoralizing."

To really connect and support, intensify your validation efforts by joining them in their reactions.

* "I would feel the same way in your shoes!"

You may even be able to share a similar experience to build camaraderie, just be careful not to hijack and make it all about you. We're going for *you're not alone* not *you're not important* here.

If you're baffled by their reaction and joining them would be dishonest (or just not possible for you), then you can lump them in with others. Again, we're going for *you're not alone.*

* "I bet your colleagues feel the same way."

Before you offer advice or try to talk them into change (e.g., changing the way they are thinking about, feeling, or approaching the situation), validate first. It's very much like the persuasion piece— demonstrate understanding so that the other person's basic need to feel seen is met, *then* they will be more amenable to help or taking effective action.

A CHALLENGE FOR YOU

I'll challenge you to do three things:

1. Pay attention to the people who you interact with that make you feel good, especially if you walk away from the interaction with a sense of *they really get me.* What did they do or say? How did they provide validation?

2. Be on the lookout for validation opportunities and try it out yourself. If this is a new skill for you, you'll probably miss the opportunities in the moment. That's okay. There's still room to grow. Reflect on interactions or conversations that involved conflict or disagreement or ones in which you found yourself giving advice or support. If you could rewind and redo, how might you alter your response to be more validating?

3. Answer this question honestly, am I validating or invalidating toward *myself*?

"The most basic of all human needs is the need to understand and be understood."

—DR. RALPH NICHOLS

WHEN HELP ISN'T SO HELPFUL

For the most part, people want to help. Mother Nature designed us to be cooperative—it enabled our survival as a species. I think that has to be why it feels good to do good. But have you ever noticed how much friction and hurt feelings sometimes arise from efforts to help?

If you've ever found yourself getting lashed out at after offering a suggestion or confusedly saying, "But I was just trying to help" to your upset loved one, then you know what I mean. If you've ever offered idea after idea, only to end up frustrated by every single one being shot down, you know what I mean. Ditto if you've ever just wanted to feel heard by the person who's busy telling you what you should do or felt annoyed while on the receiving end of unsolicited advice.

Each of these scenarios includes someone trying—and pretty much failing—to be helpful. If wanting to help others is an innate yet noble drive and if supportive caring relationships include helping each other out, why then, does help often end up being so unhelpful?

HOW OUR MINDS GET IN THE WAY

Our minds are problem-solving machines. It's difficult to overestimate how valuable this ability is... but sometimes too much of a good thing sucks.

We move through the world—and through our relationships—with that part of our minds operating like a heat-seeking missile on a mission to find "the problem." The issue is that we often miss the mark, landing on one thing we perceive to be the problem while missing the real deal.

Your partner starts venting about their frustrating day at work and a situation with their coworker. You jump in with helpful advice about how they should handle it, and your partner seems more upset. Why? You were trying to help solve the wrong problem. The real problem isn't the work situation; it's that your partner was feeling stressed and needed support.

The second problem with our problem-solving prowess is that it kicks in when it doesn't need to. We start trying to fix things that don't need to be fixed or that aren't our responsibility to take care of. This leads to giving unsolicited advice, which, while undoubtedly brilliant, is going to land like criticism or feel like pushiness. Neither of those is helpful.

The fixing things that aren't ours can also lead to over-functioning, where we step in to function on someone else's behalf, and we take on more than is necessary or healthy. While there may be some short-term payoffs, the long-term isn't good for either one of you.

Parents, you may have fallen into this trap. You, of course, help your child when they struggle with their homework. Over time, you end up doing the bulk of a project for them. After all, it's late, they need to get it done, and they can't get a bad grade. This becomes the norm as they learn you'll pick up their slack, and you keep digging yourself into the help-gone-wrong hole.

HOW TO ACTUALLY HELP

There are many, many ways to help someone... and many ways to be unhelpful. As a general framework:

1. Make sure you're clear on the problem.

Is it an inside problem (meaning feelings or thoughts or some internal struggle like being stuck in negativity) or an outside problem (the coworker, the social studies project)? If you're not sure, ask.

2. Before you jump into problem-solving mode and start offering advice or solutions (or anything involving the word "should"), ask what they need.

* "Do you need me to help you figure out a plan or just listen?"

* "Do you want to fix this or just vent?"

* "What can I do to help?"

* "What would make things better for you?"

* "Would it be helpful if I...?"

3. A bit of unsolicited advice, do NOT give unsolicited advice.

If you're convinced that your insights would make a real difference for them, at least ask if they're open to hearing some advice before giving it. Then, please, respect their wishes.

4. Sometimes it's hard to know how to help, especially if they're not sure what they need.

And, sometimes there isn't really anything you can do to help, other than offer compassion. Compassion sounds like: "Of course, you feel that way. Who wouldn't? It sucks, and I'm so sorry. I wish there was something I could do." And with that statement, you've helped. That acknowledgment and validation does more than you know.

HOW TO GET THE HELP YOU NEED

Knowing that others want to help and that it is absolutely, 100% okay to ask for, want, or truly need help (seriously, EVERYONE needs help sometimes. It's not a weakness, a burden, a failure, or a flaw. It's human.), it is sometimes up to us to take responsibility for getting the kind of help we need.

If you're not sure how to do that, in a word: Ask.

In a few more words: Ask, clearly and kindly, for the kind of help you want or need. Set the other person up for success by letting them know what the problem is and what they can do to help you.

We have a tendency to expect others who are close to us to be in tune with us. Ideally, they are. But being attuned to someone does not mean being able to read their mind. It's unreasonable to expect someone to just know what you need when you need it all the time.

Help them out by clearly telling them what you need.

For example, preface a venting session with, "I had a rough day. I just need you to listen for a bit." Then launch into the frustrating situation with your coworker. That'll cue them to sidestep the urge to share solutions or tell you what you should do.

Sometimes, we don't really know what will help. We can tell in the moment that something isn't helping but struggle to identify what would. We've probably all been there before. But, if you're not sure what you need, how can you expect someone else to know? In those times, it might be important to cut you both some slack. Recognize their efforts for what they are: a caring gesture intended to help. Even if it's misguided. Tell them you appreciate that they want to help, that you know they care, and (gently, kindly) explain why their attempts have fallen flat. And if you're the one who missed the mark, try to set frustration, powerlessness, or ego aside and realize it's not an insult. Sometimes we need to help each other help us out.

"Our prime purpose in this life is to help others."

—DALAI LAMA

WE ARE ALL CONNECTED

I happen to be in Arkansas visiting my family, and my parents were so excited that I'd be able to join them at their neighbor's Memorial Day get together. My dad, especially, gets a kick out of the fact that his neighbors are Doc and Ashley, and some of my friends have nicknamed me Doc.

"I can't wait for Doc and Ashley to meet Doc Ashley!"

Turns out, they're lovely people. Friendly and instantly likable, as were their friends and family who were also there. Good food, good people, beautiful weather, and gorgeous scenery. What a way to spend a Saturday.

MEMORIAL DAY

Memorial Day weekend is always a poignant time for me because it is the anniversary of my brother's death. As is often the case, over time, the loss has become less noticeable. The waves of grief come a lot less frequently and don't wreck me the way they used to. Still, I never quite know what to expect on this particular day.

This morning started out like any other, except that I happened to be with my other brother, Joey, soaking up some quality sibling time, which we don't often get, living in different states. I was aware of the day's significance and acknowledged it in my own way, but wasn't acutely feeling the loss.

Then there was this beautiful, overwhelming moment at Doc and Ashley's.

WE ARE ALL CONNECTED

Doc gathered everyone inside to fix plates and enjoy some food. As we stood in an impromptu circle around their kitchen and dining room, he took the opportunity to say a few words.

He started by thanking us, a group of maybe 15, for coming over. He acknowledged that Memorial Day is about remembering those we've lost in service and those we've lost in general and how our lost loved ones would want us to celebrate. He mentioned the son he lost.

My dad shared about his son.

Another woman observed that every single one of us standing there was connected by loss—she and her husband had lost their son, too. She spoke about how we have this common thread, this unspoken understanding of each other's pain, and how we help each other heal by connecting and giving hope.

Hope. That glimmer of light in the dark that lets you know you can keep moving forward.

I felt a well of emotion as I blinked back tears. What a beautiful message.

THE LESSON

As I reflect, I am struck by a fundamental truth: We need each other.

Humans are inherently social beings. We are quite literally wired for connection. We are designed in such a way, on a biological level, that we need each other, especially during hard times.

Leaning on others for support. Offering our support to others in need. Bringing out the best in each other. Cheering each other on. Acknowledging and respecting. Seeing and accepting. Extending compassion and embracing. Cooperating and helping. This is us at our best.

I recently had a conversation in my psychology practice about the importance of coming together in the wake of a death and how not having that chance to mourn collectively, to remember jointly, is a loss in and of itself. I am struck by how many people were robbed of that chance in recent years.

And I am struck by how often we feel isolated in our pain, regardless of the source, whether it's loss of a loved one, a job, health, a relationship, a goal, or an ideal. I can think of a dozen examples from as many different kinds of situations and people where it is hard to share our pain, to let others truly see what is going on and to be there for us, to take on some of the burden, knowing it isn't actually a burden. Why is it often difficult to share our pain or to sit in pain with others when that is so desperately what we need?

MEETING OUR NEEDS

I am a big believer that needs need to be honored and that problems arise when they aren't. We need to internalize the idea that love and pain, joy and sorrow, are two sides of the same coin for we cannot have one without the other. We need to be brave enough to face and explore our pain points. We need to have the courage to embrace the vulnerability required to let others see our pain. We need to acknowledge our need for help and support. We need to accept it when it is offered and seek it out when it isn't. We need to approach others with empathy, not only in their moments of vulnerability but always. We never know what someone else has gone through and what heartaches today might be bringing them.

We need each other.

"We need each other, deeper than anyone ever dares to admit even to themselves. I think it's a genetic imperative that we huddle together and hold on to each other."

—PATCH ADAMS

SECTION 4

Values, Valued, and Valuable: Who Are You and What Do You Stand for?

Who are you and what do you stand for? While it may not seem like it, those two questions are vital. Knowing who you are—what kind of person you are, what's important—*truly* important—to you, what matters, and what you want your time on this planet to be about—is like having a built-in GPS for life. Those answers guide your decisions and let you know when you're veering off course.

In psychology, we call those your personal values... and most people don't actually have a good sense of theirs unless they've done some serious work to sort it out.

There's no one right way to figure out your values. It's a winding path and an ongoing process. Sometimes, if we pause and reflect, we can get a sense of *Yes! This is me* or *This is what I want to be about.*

Other times, we find out who we are through what we go through. We are shaped by our experiences, both good and bad. Success and adversity can show us who we are... or who we don't want to be. In turn, leaning on our values—staying true to ourselves—in the face of challenge can help us be strong and resilient.

Courage, curiosity, and compassion. Those are my guiding principles, and I try to embody them in whatever I do. I am grateful that
the nature of my job has encouraged me to do that work—I mean,
how hypocritical would it be of me to tell others to find and follow
their values if I didn't do it myself?

Now it's your turn.

WHERE ARE YOU GOING IN LIFE?

I spent a couple years in Omaha in my late 20s. When my friend Marcel came to visit toward the end of my tenure there, he suggested that we go explore downtown.

"Where do you want to go?" I asked.

"Let's just explore," he replied.

Just explore. Park the car. Get out. Wander around with no specific agenda, entering places as we passed them, checking out what the area had to offer, staying as long as it struck our fancy and moving on when we felt ready. I learned more about Omaha in that weekend than in the entire time I had lived there. Marcel opened my eyes to a new way of approaching life, one of exploration, of being curious, of being open, of almost expecting to find treasures if only you're willing to look for them.

In the years since, one of my favorite games has become what I call Left, Right, Straight. Whether it's in my own neighborhood, another part of my city, or a new location all together, I find it fun to approach each intersection with the question, "Left, right, or straight?" Then I go with my gut, and let chance call the shots. By allowing myself to be open to exploring, to getting lost, to wandering aimlessly, I have stumbled upon some really cool finds that I would have missed otherwise. In my own Kansas City, I found hidden gems like beautiful buildings and great shrimp tacos, free back-alley concerts, a book fair with local authors, and fire dancers. In Puerto Viejo, I found this amazing jungle trail right next to the beach that became my favorite walking path. In other cities, I've found the best passionfruit daiquiris, a beach cove with a glorious sunset view, street musicians, graffiti murals, impromptu rap battles, galleries, the most absolutely adorable red trench coat that I never knew I needed, and more amazing meals than I can recall.

In short, I've had so many unexpected special experiences and moments of pleasure because of random chance combined with a willingness to wander, with an air of curiosity but no goal other than seeing what unfolds before me.

To be fair, I have also had some letdowns and missed opportunities with Left, Right, Straight. Like the time I ended up eating mediocre soup from a knockoff Panera at a shopping center in Chicago (Chicago! Seriously, how many incredible culinary options are there in that city?!) because my wanderings took me way far from anything else. Probably more often, though, it's not a letdown, per se. It's just... *meh*. Nothing new or particularly interesting. Nothing memorable. Just lots of time being lost and lots of lost time. Yet, I continue to embrace the game.

As I was playing recently, letting my mind wander where it wanted as my body did the same, I thought about this game as a metaphor for life. How often do we wander aimlessly? When is that a good thing and when is it not? What's the balance between exploring and allowing life to surprise you versus marking your destination and charting your course straight toward it?

WHEN YOU'RE LOST

I've spent a lot of time in life being lost, both literally and metaphorically. Back when I still drove, though I was able to see well enough to operate a moving vehicle, I wasn't typically able to read a lot of the street signs, which meant I frequently missed my turn. Most of the time, it was no big deal. I recognized almost immediately that I had made a mistake and could easily get back on track. Sometimes, though, not so much, especially in the days before GPS. More than once, I ended up in unfamiliar territory completely turned around. Yet, somehow, I always managed to get where I needed to go. Even when I was hopelessly lost, when I might as well have been playing Left, Right, Straight because it was a complete guess which direction would put me back on course, I could continue, correcting and adjusting with each turn or stopping to ask for directions until I found my way.

Because I got a lot of practice with it, I got pretty comfortable being lost. I learned to trust that I'd eventually find my way. Even in life, when I have periods of feeling lost, I know that I can get back to my true North.

We can't do that, though, if we don't know what our true North is.

That's why it's important to take the time in self-reflection to get clear on who you are and where you want to go with your life. What matters to you? What do you want to be defined by? What parameters are plotting your course? Without that, you're playing a lifelong version of Left, Right, Straight and hoping that you get lucky enough to stumble across something worthwhile. Maybe you will... and maybe you'll end up with mediocre soup.

STAY THE COURSE OR VENTURE INTO UNCHARTED WATERS?

We need to do both. Having a direction in life helps guide the choices we make and the steps we take. It keeps us from wandering aimlessly, squandering our precious gift of time. Sometimes, though, being too myopic means missing out on the wonderful treasures that life has to offer. There is value in exploring, in playing life's version of Left, Right, Straight to see what we encounter and what we learn from those new experiences.

WHAT HAPPENS WHEN YOU GET MISGUIDED?

One day in San Jose, Costa Rica, my friend Natalie and I decided we were going to adventure and explore. We had a destination in mind—the National Theater—but no timeline for getting there. We knew the general direction we needed to go—toward the city center—so we hopped on a bus heading that direction and hopped off when it looked like we were getting close. It worked out beautifully.

The return trip was a different story. There were dozens of buses in the city center, all heading to different parts of the city. In our limited Spanish, we asked bystanders and bus drivers, "Are you heading west?" the direction toward our Airbnb. After tons of confused looks, head shakes, and nos, one driver just smiled and said, "Get on." We breathed a sigh of relief as we took our seats.

Thanks to technology, we could see our location on a map in real time. We watched, alternating between relief and anxiety, as we alternated between heading west, then turning south. Then west again, and then south. *Should we keep going? Should we get off?* Finally, when we turned east, we realized we were heading way off course. It was dark, in an unfamiliar city, and we didn't know where this bus would end up. It wasn't the time for Left, Right, Straight. We hit the stop button, got off, and went with Plan B, calling an Uber.

I took the lesson as this: explore, especially when you have the time and the opportunity. Don't be afraid to try something that you're not sure will work out. But, ultimately, have a clear enough sense of where you want to go that you can hop off the bus when it's going the wrong way. Even when others tell you, "This is the right bus. This is where you need to go or what you need to do," know that they might be wrong. Perhaps it's right for them, yet it might be wrong for you. Know yourself and your true North. Then, trust yourself. And be willing to get off the bus in the middle of nowhere to get back on track when you need to.

With that, I'll leave you with some questions to consider. What are your guiding principles? Your personal GPS coordinates, if you will? How do you know when you're having fun playing Left, Right, Straight about to be delighted by something unexpected and when you are just squandering time wandering aimlessly? Worse, do you know when you are on the wrong bus? And when you realize that you are, do you have the courage to hop off and find a way to get back?

"The wisest men follow their own direction."

—EURIPIDES

LIVE FOR YOUR EULOGY

My sweet great-aunt Betty died a few years ago, during COVID. She was a loving woman living on borrowed time, a light in this world for nearly nine decades. Thanks to technology, I was able to attend her funeral virtually. As I listened to the beautiful eulogy my cousin delivered, I was struck by how perfectly he captured her life and just how richly she embodied the things that were important to her.

And it made me think of my own eulogy.

As morbid as it might sound, I've given some serious thought over the years to what I hope people will say about me when I'm gone, and I urge you to do the same.

Imagining your own eulogy helps you get a clear vision of the kind of person you want to be and the kind of mark you want to leave on this world. In a sense, it becomes your road map through life, your personal guide for how to live *your* good life.

In the weeks following my aunt's passing, I realized that if I were to die today, I'm not sure that my aspirational eulogy would fit. As much as I think about and talk about living your values and intentionally cultivating a good life, my actions of late have fallen short.

That's a tough pill to swallow.

I think the toll of disrupted routines, social distancing limitations, and the constant loom of impending crises made life feel less vibrant for many of us. I don't know about you, but it hasn't been a recipe for always showing up the way I want to.

I am fortunate, though, that it's not too late to course correct. I am humbled and reminded that psychological strength, which helps me live my eulogy, is not a one time, check-it-off-the-list achievement kind of thing. It requires ongoing and intentional practice. I don't have to wait for anything external to change, though. I simply have to make the choice to begin again, right now, and to do the work.

If you, too, have gotten away from living your eulogy—or even if you haven't quite figured out what your life is all about yet—it's not too late for you, either. Let's commit, today, to embody the qualities that matter most to us.

"In the end, it's not the years in your life that count. It's the life in your years."
—ABRAHAM LINCOLN

THE SECRET SAUCE OF SELF-IMPROVEMENT

Yesterday, I recorded some video content for a project I'm working on. I did dozens of takes of various segments to give myself lots of footage to choose from. After a couple hours, I called it a wrap and headed home. I started reviewing clips only to realize that my hair was sticking up crazy in several of them, rendering them useless, and (please don't judge), I mixed up the start and stop recording buttons on several more, ending up with random shots of the wall and floor as I positioned the camera. While I'm hoping to still find some usable bits, there's a decent chance that my efforts were wasted... all because I failed to stop and reflect.

A quick little peek at my reflection in the mirror would've solved the hair situation, and a periodic pause to watch, or at least spot check, my recordings would've prevented the second snafu. Instead, I barreled through my plan without some much needed and valuable awareness.

Now, extend my day yesterday into a metaphor for life. What happens when you barrel through it without pausing to take stock? How can you grow or improve in some way if you don't take the time to establish a good baseline and regularly monitor how you're doing? How can you exercise choice when you're moving through life on autopilot? We all need a strong sense of self-awareness, which hinges on being able to self-reflect.

THE IMPORTANCE OF SELF-REFLECTION

Can you imagine moving through a single day without at least checking your reflection in the mirror? Probably not. Most of us feel more comfortable with at least a cursory glance to make sure we're presentable, especially if we're going to be out and about in the world.

Self-reflection is like holding up a mirror to your thoughts, emotions, and behaviors so that you can take a good, hard look at them and determine if they're okay or need some work.

Without intentional self-reflection, it's hard to really recognize patterns or habits, leaving us doomed to repeat them. Even if we realize that we have some problematic patterns, say in relationships or reacting to triggers, we are not able to truly change them without the self-awareness that arises from self-reflection.

WHAT, EXACTLY, IS SELF-REFLECTION?

Self-reflection is the act of pausing, stepping back, and considering your reactions—what you did and how you felt—and the factors that led to or contributed to them. It's the process of uncovering your underlying motivations and the inner workings of your mind that drive your reactions.

Self-reflection is a skill, and one that many people either don't have or don't use. If you're sitting here, however, thinking *this doesn't apply to me. I self-reflect. All. The. Time.* Good for you, but hang with me. There's some stuff coming up that might apply to you.

HOW TO SELF-REFLECT

There are a lot of ways to practice self-reflection. As long as you are trying to objectively analyze how and why you reacted the way you did or do the things you do, you're self-reflecting. This may be a quiet, introspective process for you, one in which you simply think through your reactions. You may also find that a more structured method is better for you, especially if this is a new skill.

Self-monitoring is a tool that psychologists use all the time to help increase awareness of problematic patterns, habits and behaviors, or internal experiences like thoughts, feelings, and urges. One way to do this is to make note of the ABCs of your behavior or reaction any time it happens.

A stands for antecedents and captures anything leading up to your reaction. B is the behavior itself. C is the consequence or the outcome. Think of it like a chain of events, and the more detailed the better.

Often, people miss the internal experiences—the inner workings of their mind—that are really important to understand. To do this, after the fact, take a few minutes to note the situation/trigger/context. Then, try to identify your internal experiences: thoughts, emotions, physical sensations inside your body, and urges for action. Finally, reflect on the outcome. The goal is to fill in the gap between what happened and how you behaved. You can download a version of this exercise I call Dissecting the Problem at www.drashleysmith.com/the-way-I-see-it-tools.

Journaling is another way that some people self-reflect. Allowing yourself to write out what you're thinking or feeling, then reading back through it, may shed some light on your inner workings or motivations.

Talking with a therapist or a trusted confidant who can ask probing questions without you feeling defensive or avoidant can also promote self-reflection.

Finally, mindfulness is another powerful way to develop moment-to-moment self-awareness as you become better able to watch internal experiences unfold, rather than being ruled by them like when we're moving through life on autopilot.

WHEN SELF-REFLECTION GOES AWRY

There can be a fine line between self-reflection and self-criticism or ruminating, so let's distinguish them for the record. Some of the key differences between effective self-reflection and unhelpful self-focused thinking have to do with attitude, goals, and utility.

Approach self-reflection with an attitude of curiosity. *Hmmm, what was it that made me feel that way, I wonder? I wonder what made me do that. I wonder what old script my mind was running.* Contrast that to self-criticism, which operates from a judgmental attitude. *Why did I do that?* Asked with an undertone of judgment and the strong message that you shouldn't have or that you did something wrong.

Self-reflection has the goal of helping to increase our self-awareness and our understanding of how we tick, with the ultimate goals of growth, improvement, or self-acceptance. Self-criticism, on the other hand, has the goal of making us feel so bad we won't do it again... except that we will because we didn't get useful information we can use in the future.

The utility is different between the two as well. Self-reflection can be painful at times, but it provides a path forward. It is constructive and yields useful information. Self-criticism, on the other hand, leads to guilt, shame, and/or anxiety. It might provide some (at least initial) motivation to change, but it doesn't shed light on how to actually do that, other than vague demands to do better or be better.

Rumination is chewing on negative thoughts, looping or spiraling. Think of self-reflection as more of a discrete exercise. Go through the process—check your reflection in the mirror—then move on. Rumination is like looking in the mirror... then leaning in close and honing in on all the things you don't like about what you see, fixating on how bad or ugly they are. You can lose hours like that and be far worse off for it.

The takeaway here is to reflect in a helpful way, use that information to cultivate self-awareness, and build on that awareness in the moment to make helpful changes or break old patterns that no longer serve you.

Me? I'll be taking the time to do a little more reflection along the way. While it may take a few extra minutes that I don't want to spend or feel kind of cringy in the moment, it's far better than causing unintended consequences or problems, like my unusable footage.

"Without reflection, we go blindly on our way, creating more unintended consequences, and failing to achieve anything useful."

—MARGARET J. WHEATLE

CHANNEL YOUR INNER TAYLOR SWIFT: FINDING THE INSPIRATION TO BE WHO YOU WANT TO BE

I grew up dancing ballet, a technically rigid style of movement taught by an exacting teacher. There was a precise position for each part of your body in each and every move, a standard of perfection to strive for. It wasn't all that different when I shifted to ballroom dancing as an adult.

And then I found swing dancing.

While West Coast Swing has a structure and basic technique, it allows for much more creative expression and personal style. Champion-level swing dancers range from what you'd envision a dancer to look like—young and lithe—to middle-aged seemingly out-of-shape people, and every one puts their own unique twist on the dance. It's one of the things I love about it... and one of the things I struggled with initially.

Until that point, as a dancer, I'd had in mind that there was one objectively correct way to execute a move. Swing challenged me to be more flexible and to expand my definition of right. It was initially uncomfortable but ultimately freeing.

STEPPING INTO SOMEONE'S SILHOUETTE

My first ballroom and swing instructor, Matt, introduced this concept he called stepping into someone's silhouette. It was a way to emulate someone else's style. By that, he meant envisioning the shape of your idol's body and the quality of their movement, then mimicking it by trying to create the same silhouette. It made sense to me at the time, and I practiced trying on styles, attempting to embody them until I found the one that fit for me.

I think this concept applies far beyond the dance floor.

CHANNEL YOUR INNER TAYLOR SWIFT

One way humans learn is through observing others and imitating what we see, what psychologists call the Social Learning Theory. We learn all manner of things by looking to others as guides, not only as children trying to figure out how to operate in this world, but as adults, too, whether we realize it or not.

I talked to a college student recently who was telling me about some drama in her friend group. She told me how she was channeling Michelle Obama and Taylor Swift as inspiration for taking the high road and keeping things classy rather than resorting to being petty or passive aggressive. I thought it was such a brilliant take on the old "be the bigger person" advice. Intentionally following in her icons' footsteps allowed her to forego the immediate satisfaction that comes from going off on someone who wronged you and, ultimately, helped her navigate the challenging group dynamics in a way that left her without regret.

VALUES BOARD OF DIRECTORS

There are a number of reasons why having official and unofficial mentors can be beneficial. They help you develop skills, rise through the ranks in your career, pave the way in other journeys like parenting and fitness. But one way mentors can be especially helpful is by modeling the kind of human being you want to be.

Dr. April, my co-founder at Peak Mind, introduced me to this great exercise called Your Values Board of Directors. Think of five people, either in your real life or from afar, who you admire for the way they behave and the way they move through the world. Then, think about the qualities they exhibit that draw you to them. Alternatively, you can think about how you would like to be then find people who exemplify those traits.

Do you want to go high when they go low like Mrs. Obama? Shake it off like T Swift? Exude patience? Be bold and decisive? Authentic? Creative? Intelligent? Funny? Strong? In what ways?

Once you've identified people who exhibit these qualities, mentally invite them to join your Values Board of Directors. Then, look to them for inspiration and guidance when challenging situations arise. Ask yourself, "WWTD (What would Taylor do)?" Imagine how they would respond in the face of whatever frustration, disappointment, setback, or opportunity it is that you are encountering. Step into their silhouette, so to speak, and see how it feels for you as a person and how it plays out.

"No matter what happens in life, be good to people. Being good to people is a wonderful legacy to leave behind."

—TAYLOR SWIFT

THE POWER OF PATIENCE

We've all heard the saying "patience is a virtue." I'll be honest, though, it's not a sexy, snazzy one. It doesn't conjure up strong, powerful images like courage or wisdom do. It doesn't seem big like creativity or boldness. Instead, patience calls to mind slowness or tranquility. It can almost feel meek or subdued.

It's a mistake to view patience that way. It is actually incredibly underrated. Patience is powerful. So many things in life can be improved by mastering this essential skill.

HOLD YOUR HORSES

Unless you find yourself in the ER, the OR, or work as a first responder, I'd dare to say that very few things are truly life or death. Yet, we treat them like a crisis, unable (unwilling?) to exercise patience... often to our detriment.

* The person you're dating goes out with their friends and doesn't text you back. You get anxious or angry, check your phone constantly, and maybe rapid-fire messages you later regret when you find out their phone died.

* Your kid comes home from school crying about someone being mean to them. Your mama bear instincts kick in, and you

call the other kid's mom to demand action... before finding out the whole story and how your child instigated it.

* You embark on a journey of self-improvement. Frustrated by the slow pace of progress, you inadvertently sabotage things by biting off more than you can chew or, alternatively, giving up.

* You hear rumors of layoffs coming down the pike. Anxious and consumed by a need to know, you're too distracted by talking about whether your job is safe or not that you can't even do said job.

* You interrupt your partner because you just know what they're going to say... and the argument escalates.

Countless examples abound. Times when we feel a sense of urgency or frustration with waiting. We struggle to pause, practice patience, and allow things to unfold, potentially even resolving on their own. And in rushing to action in our impatience, we often make things worse.

WHY IS IT SO HARD TO BE PATIENT?

Patience seems to be in short supply for many people these days, in part because of the way our brains work and in part because of our modern lifestyles. As technology has improved, our ability to wait has gone the other direction. Thanks to Google, we now expect to have answers immediately and have little tolerance for not knowing or having to do the leg work to find out. Same-day delivery makes waiting weeks for whatever goody caught our eye seem unacceptable. We take for granted that we can have what we want when we want it, and the effect isn't flattering. We get angry when things are delayed. We get anxious sitting in the not knowing. We even get bored or defeated way too soon.

Short Attention Spans

It seems that technology and the pace of life have conspired to zap our attention spans. We expect big flashy things to grab and hold our attention and move on in mere seconds if they don't. Contrast TikTok videos with reading a book or compare current day news, with its striking headlines and super short stories, to the long-form, no bells and whistles news of a generation ago. We want immediate entertainment, easy and instantaneous engagement, and have zero patience with waiting for the real substance.

Delayed Gratification Is Hard

Similarly, we expect instant results in our lives. We see others having success, whether that's in relationships, business, or health, and we want the same. Right. Now. And when those results don't come immediately, it's easy to give up rather than be patient with the process. Change can take time. Success must be built, not willed into existence.

Anxiety and Urgency

Beyond the I-want-it-now-and-waiting-is-unacceptable phenomenon, we also have to consider how a sense of urgency makes it hard to be patient. Anxiety, our body's built-in threat detection system, does several things in an attempt to keep us safe. One of those is to up the sense of urgency.

Anxiety makes whatever it is focused on feel important. *This is a big deal, and it must be dealt with right this second.* Moreover, anxiety constricts our attention so that the perceived threat is all we can focus on. That also ups the sense of urgency. And anxiety is demanding by nature. It literally compels us to handle the threat—remove it, escape it, avoid it, and don't stop thinking about it until you do. Anxiety turns things into crises... but they aren't.

Again, unless it's truly life or death, it isn't the crisis it feels like. I promise.

Even looming deadlines with very real implications for your professional or personal life or someone you care about being in pain (like your child crying or your friend struggling), while important and maybe even urgent, aren't a crisis. We can practice patience and address what needs to be done effectively, from a place of calm, self-control. We don't have to run around frantically like a chicken with its head cut off.

Intolerance of Distress

Finally, our intolerance of distress often drives us to be impatient... and impulsive. In psychology, this term means being unable or unwilling to experience distress or discomfort. Again, we have a sense of urgency. *I want to feel better right now. I want this to go away right now. I can't handle this for a single second longer.*

Those imperatives often lead to ineffective or even destructive behaviors. Not a great way to go through life given that we will inevitably experience distress or discomfort, probably pretty often. Instead, we need patience, among other things, to be able to tolerate the "ick" without making it worse.

HOW TO BECOME MORE PATIENT

Patience is the ability to handle delays or challenges in a calm, composed manner rather than reacting with anger, anxiety, or impulsivity. It's not something that comes naturally to most people. Rather, it's something that has to be developed and practiced.

Patience isn't something you either have or don't. It's a skill, albeit a complex one, that can be mastered.

If patience isn't your strong suit, I implore you to start doing the work. Use these tips to help you practice.

1. Adopt the right mindset

You need to believe that patience is a good thing. You need to believe that you are (or can become) a patient person. And you need to approach things from a patient perspective, intentionally setting the goal of practicing patience.

2. Pause

When you feel yourself getting impatient—anxious or angry about having to wait for something you want (whether that's answers, relief, or results)—pause. Literally and figuratively. Be still. Stop talking.

3. Take a breath or two

I know, I know. It's annoying to be told to take a deep breath, especially when you're feeling agitated and have that sense of urgency telling you that you don't have time. You have time to breathe. You're going to do it anyways, so at least make it useful. Take a full inhale—feel your belly fill, your chest expand, and take air in all the way up to your collarbone. Then, exhale slowly. Deep breaths, especially with a longer exhale than inhale, tell your body to chill out. It's a mini-reset. Repeat it often.

4. Be a good coach for yourself

Use your self-talk intentionally. Notice and describe what is happening internally. Think of it like being a narrator. *I feel impatient. I feel annoyed and worried. I have a strong urge to address this now.* Then, coach yourself to be patient. *I want to fix this now, but there is no need to be impulsive. I can practice patience. I will wait and see how things play out. It will likely be fine. This is not a crisis.*

I repeat. This is not a crisis.

5. Move with ease

When we feel impatient, it shows up in our movements. We move with frenetic energy and tension. Instead, slow it down. Relax your muscles and move as though you feel patient, even if you don't.

What other psychological strength skills or strategies can you use to tap into the power of patience?

"If I don't have patience, then the problem gets bigger instead of smaller."

—LEAH, age 8, in *Magnolia Magazine*

HOW TO STAY BALANCED AND FOCUSED IN LIFE

I am fresh off the yoga mat, after an invigorating flow class that left me feeling sweaty, limber, strong, and centered; it's all of the things I love about this practice.

I've been practicing yoga, with more and less consistency depending on the phase of life, since I was 14, thanks to a mom who got into it before it was cool. I've always appreciated it as an exercise form and what it can do to shape my physical body. In more recent years, though, as I've embraced mindfulness and meditation, I value that aspect of yoga as well. The physical and mental benefits of pairing breath with movement are why yoga is a central part of my self-care routine.

Despite the countless hours on the mat, I've done incredibly little work to learn the philosophical underpinnings of the practice and, if I'm being honest, tend to inwardly roll my eyes when teachers start talking about woo-woo nonsense.

And yet, yoga has survived thousands of years. There are lessons from the mat beyond body alignment and how to regulate your breathing that really do translate to successful modern living.

One is the importance of a drishti.

UNWAVERING FOCUS

One of my favorite parts about yoga has always been balance poses. These challenging postures require strength and balance in order to execute them, particularly for any length of time. The secret? Finding a drishti.

A drishti is simply a focal point.

Teachers advise us novice yogis to find something to focus on that isn't moving. That means not looking at another human because even the teacher is going to wobble. Keeping your gaze solidly on your drishti aids tremendously in being able to balance. When your eyes dart around, your balance fails. And even if your eyes stay still but your attention wanders, you'll fall out of the pose, too.

I think I've intuitively liked balance work because of the forced mindfulness, even before I knew that's what I was doing. But now, I find the concept of a drishti more wide-reaching than I originally realized.

As I bobbled on the mat today, trying to regain my balance and focus, I thought about how important it is to have a drishti in life (ironic that these musings kept me from staying focused in the moment).

We need to have a focal point—something to hold on to, to orient toward. Like a sea captain using the North Star to stay on course, we need our own unwavering marker to keep us moving in the right direction and let us know when we're beginning to drift off course.

I've noticed that when I'm not focused on my metaphorical drishti, it's easy for me to flounder. I can get distracted by others' movements and feel like I need to be going in the same direction, only to be distracted by something that pulls me in yet another.

As I try to grow various aspects of my business, I am constantly bombarded by messaging that is loud and competing for my time, attention, and energy. You need SEO! No, grow your social media presence. It's all about sales. Don't miss the ChatGPT and AI revolution. Focus on networking and relationships. Email marketing is where it's at.

It's overwhelming.

And I notice that when I get hooked by each shiny thing, each important ball that I'm dropping, each promised path to success, I feel like I'm bouncing around aimlessly, lost at sea. I'm doing a lot of things but I don't feel balanced, solid, or grounded. That's when I know I need to come back to my drishti. I need to refocus on MY North Star. My values and goals. And that means tuning out the distractions.

It's one thing to look to others who are ahead of you on your path to find guidance and inspiration—why reinvent the wheel if you don't have to? But looking to others who aren't on the same path you want to be on only opens you up to being pulled off course.

If your drishti as a parent is raising compassionate, resilient little humans, then tune out the Pinterest-fueled guilt trips and focus on what matters. If your drishti at this point in life is improving your health, tune out the invitations for patio happy hours. If your drishti is financial security, say no to keeping up with Joneses. Find your drishti, lock onto it, and stay focused and balanced.

WHAT TO DO WHEN YOU FALL

One day at yoga, I had my drishti. My mind was focused, but the balance pose was a bigger challenge than my body could successfully navigate (yet). Starting in a runner's lunge, we hooked our big toes with our peace fingers, extended our legs out as we rotated our bodies into a side plank. It was every bit as difficult as it sounds. It required strength, flexibility, AND balance... and I fell out of the pose multiple times.

Another lesson I've learned on the mat is to laugh when that happens. As one of my teachers reminds us often: "Humans wobble. Embrace the wobble."

We must hold lightly to our goals, learn to approach life with levity, and to laugh when we fall. The alternative is to set rigidly high standards that leave us feeling like failures when we miss the mark, which we inevitably will.

I don't know about you, but I would rather find the humor, shake it off, and jump right back in, learning and adjusting based on my previous failures, until I nail what I'm going for.

I think being able to embrace the wobbles while staying focused on my drishti is the way to go. It's the key to staying balanced and focused and to righting the ship when it teeters or veers off course.

Namaste.

"The myth is that there isn't enough time. There is plenty of time. There isn't enough focus with the time you have. You win by directing your attention toward better things."

—JAMES CLEAR

WHICH IS MORE IMPORTANT, THE JOURNEY OR THE DESTINATION?

"Are we there yet?" I asked/whined.

"Ashley, it's been like five minutes since you asked last time. What's with the ants in the pants?" she replied, with only the slightest touch of detectable annoyance. (Her patience was commendable.)

I wish I could say this was a conversation between childhood Ashley and her parent, but the reality is this was well into adulthood, on a road trip with my best friend, Natalie.

I was really excited to get where we were going, and that forward-focused anticipation made it tough to just relax and enjoy the short trip. In a way, it made the experience more stressful and definitely more unpleasant than it had to be... for both of us.

THE ING V. THE ED

You know how it feels when someone drops some insight that rocks your world? It's as though something clicks into place and things all of a sudden make so much more sense. And *then*, you try to share your new wisdom with someone else, and it comes out kind of garbled, falling pretty short of sparking those same lightbulbs for them?

I'm afraid this is going to be one of those times.

In a recent session, my coach, Shannon, worked her usual magic, and I left feeling like I had a solid understanding of what I was experiencing and, more importantly, actionable wisdom to follow when I start to veer off course again.

We talked about the Ing v. the Ed.

Not to be confused with the *id*, Freud's pleasure-seeking part of consciousness.

Ed, as in past-tense. WalkED, presentED, pitchED, dancED. Focusing on the Ed means focusing on the final outcome, on what happens after you do the thing.

In contrast, the Ing is the process, the doING. PreparING, writING, learnING, collaboratING, dancING. It places the emphasis on the process of what you are doing, rather than on the outcome or the end result.

This conversation came about because I have some lofty goals but was noticing that I was feeling stressed, behind, and overwhelmed. My headspace was becoming busier and more negative than I like it to be, and I was having a hard time moving forward in a way that felt calm and confident.

She helped me figure out that I was getting caught up in the Ed. I was thinking about how my projects will land, how others will react to them, whether they'll be successful by whatever external metrics apply.

I was thinking ahead in a not so helpful way.

I don't want to abandon these goals. They are important to me for a variety of reasons and are things that I genuinely want to pour my time, attention, and energy into. I also don't want to be a stressed-out mess in the pursuit of them, nor do I want undue stress to get in the way of me making progress. I don't want to gauge my success based on external measures—other people's reactions, the number of likes or sales I get—because when I start to go down that line of thinking, I've noticed that it zaps creativity.

All of a sudden, I'm second-guessing what I write or the decisions I make. I fall into comparisons, doubt, or procrastination. Those things make it exponentially harder to do the work I want to do.

The alternative? Focusing on the Ing. It feels qualitatively different when I am staying grounded in the present, focusing on what's important to me and why, yet holding lightly to outcomes, embracing an experimental, playful mindset instead.

It's the last road trip I did—three times longer in the car yet zero complaints. We chatted, laughed, debated nerdy topics, and didn't even pull out the audiobook we had in reserve.

Instead of "Are we there yet?" followed by scrutiny and evaluation, predictions and anticipation, it was embracing the journey—being present in the process and trusting that I'll get where I'm going—I'll hit the target goal—in due time.

IT'S ALL ABOUT THE JOURNEY

Sometimes, the actions we take are going to be the same, but it's the *experience* of doing that action—or our way of *being* while *doing*—that is different.

It's two kids in the back of a minivan headed to Disney World. One is constantly checking the time, complaining about boredom, pulling a Past Ashley and demanding, "Are we there yet?" The other watches out the window, noticing the beauty in the landscape, reading an epic fantasy novel, and being patient. Both get to Disney World at the same time, but who had a better experience?

It's begrudgingly doing the dishes, focusing on how you're the only one in the family who does them, getting mired in resentment as you think about how no one is even going to notice and say thank you. Contrast that to doing those same dishes, while focusing on how this small act is one you do to take care of your family, which is a high-level priority to you.

In both of these, the same actions happen—travel and washing—and yet the experiences are dramatically different. It's the Ing v. the Ed. The journey versus the destination.

RECOGNIZING WHEN YOU'RE OFF COURSE

As I strive to find the balance of pursuing ambitious goals while also enjoying my day-to-day life experience, I am tuning into what's driving me and why. I am trying to stay grounded in the journey, in the Ing, because those aspects are more in my control and make a huge difference, but it's hard to sidestep getting caught up in outcomes.

It's not that outcomes don't matter. It's just that they're not always in our direct control. And trying to ensure that we get the outcomes we really want can actually hold us back from taking action. If there's so much pressure on what you're doing that it seems like any misstep is a potential catastrophe, it can be hard to muster the energy (and courage) to take any step forward.

As I've gotten better at differentiating where I'm operating from, here's what I've noticed:

ING – I give myself permission to trust myself, making the decisions that feel right, knowing that I can always have a do over later.

ED – I get caught up in thinking about how the end result is going to be received, and I feel almost paralyzed with my next step. Is it right? Is it going to fail? What if it's dumb? What if I spend all this time and no one even appreciates it? Will I be humiliated? Filled with regret?

ING – feels expansive, like I am growing.

ED – feels constrictive, like I'm being squeezed in a vice or getting stuck or weighed down.

ING – I am being driven by my values and strengths.

ED – I am being driven by fear or avoidance of negative things like rejection and failure.

As you tackle your to do list, the day-to-day administrations of life, and your audacious goals, pay attention to the journey. How can you show up and be here, right where you are? How might you connect with your why? How can you move forward from a place of grounded values rather than fear or stress?

"Focus on the journey, not the destination. Joy is found not in finishing the activity but in doing it."
—GREG ANDERSON

HOW A SKINNED KNEE MADE ME GRATEFUL

I have to share a painful/slightly hilarious story with you. I was training for my first half-marathon. I was a little over seven miles into my planned eight-mile run, and I was feeling *good*. Really good, in fact, so I picked up the pace. I crossed 75th Street, the busiest intersection on my route, and the next thing I know, my face was plummeting toward the ground.

What's happening?

I'm falling

This is bad!

My face is going to hit the pavement.

Images of teeth shattering

I'm hurt!

Those were the thoughts that blinked through my mind in a jumbled instant.

Thankfully, I was able to stop my momentum at the last second, with my face hovering an inch above the ground, teeth intact. Stunned, I pushed myself up as a red minivan pulled into the near-by parking lot, presumably to make sure I was okay. (Did I mention it was a busy intersection? There were SO MANY cars stopped at the light, witnessing my fall.)

Then, another thought entered my mind: *You fell. You can't run anymore.*

Fortunately, I was able to set that thought aside before it could take hold. I quickly assessed the damage, realized I was shaken but not seriously injured, got up, and finished my run. I even beat my goal time.

I was on a path I'd traversed 100 times. I didn't feel myself trip or stumble. I didn't see it coming. Yet, I fell. Hard. And it sucked. And I got back up and persevered.

As I finished my run and then bandaged myself up at home, I reflected on what happened, and this is where the real gratitude came in.

I was tremendously grateful to my Past Self for all the hard work she's done to build psychological strength. That work was the reason I was able to get up and move forward so quickly. I had my eye on the goal and a clear sense of who I am.

- I'm the kind of person who can handle painful things.

- I'm the kind of person who doesn't let my mind take me off course.

- I'm the kind of person who isn't afraid of failure.

I CAN HANDLE PAINFUL THINGS.

I don't *like* pain. I mean, who does? Yet, aspects of psychological strength help me move through painful experiences without getting crushed. This time, it was my mindfulness (observing the present as it actually is) and acceptance (knowing that it is what it is without willing it to be different) skills that allowed me to notice and assess the painful sensations throughout my body without my mind turning up the pain volume. I didn't realize when I started cultivating these particular skills, just how crucial and widely applicable they'd be.

I DON'T LET MY MIND TAKE ME OFF COURSE.

Minds are masterful excuse generators. They are SO GOOD at making up reasons and giving us justifications for not doing hard or uncomfortable things. Part of the psych strength work I've been focusing on lately is noticing when my mind is giving me those excuses, even the really plausible, completely rational sounding ones like, "You just fell. You can't run anymore."

The reality is, I was stunned, slightly embarrassed, and in pain, but I wasn't really injured. I saw the Excuse Generator for what it was and quelled it before it even had a chance to really get going.

I AM NOT AFRAID OF FAILURE.

This one hasn't always been true for me. As a (mostly) recovered perfectionist, I've had to do a lot of work to redefine my relationship with failure so that it doesn't hold me back, and it's an ongoing process. Even after all the work I've done, deep down I still don't like being wrong, making mistakes, or failing. It's disappointing, and it hurts, especially when you're feeling really confident and don't see it coming.

That said, I am getting much better at picking myself up, dusting myself off, and persevering despite bruises (to my body or my ego). I'm steadily working on becoming the kind of person who is not afraid to falter, who can own mistakes without internal angst, and who can even find the humor in my biggest fails.

I AM GRATEFUL.

So, here I am, a 40-year-old woman with a bandaged-up skinned knee and a deep sense of gratitude. I am grateful for the work I've done to build my psychological strength, for the community who supports my journey, and for the opportunity to help others.

"Failures are like skinned knees, painful but superficial."

—ROSS PEROT

FROM TRAGEDY TO TRIUMPH

"I acquired my disability in 2012," he began.

I was speaking with Wesley Hamilton, the Executive Director and Founder of the non-profit Disabled But Not Really (DBNR). I found out about DBNR a couple weeks ago and reached out to explore possibilities for getting involved. Wes and I met by Zoom to feel each other out, and he shared his powerful story with me.

He went on to explain that he was shot by a man he did not know, resulting in a spinal cord injury that left him permanently paralyzed from the waist down. After multiple surgeries and almost two years of nearly constant bed rest, his life shifted in a big way.

He lost more than 100 pounds, a feat he did not think was possible for him even prior to injury. He began to strength train and became an award-winning adaptive athlete. His self-concept changed. His mindset was on point, and he became determined to help others realize that disability is not a death sentence.

His work to establish and grow DBNR has been incredible. He's made a tangible, unquantifiable impact on the lives of so many individuals, while scaling a non-profit and making splashes in national media.

I was impressed and inspired.

And then he said something that gave me chill bumps: "The man who shot me tried to take my life... but really, he gave it to me."

Wow.

WEATHERING THE STORM

Last weekend, massive, atypical storms blew through Kansas City. I was lucky. My power came back on within a few hours, and the huge tree in my front yard barely shed. In contrast, many of my fellow Kansas Citians were left with giant trees felled in their yards or on their homes and downed power lines that disrupted electricity and internet service for days. My friends, neighbors, and community rose the next day to begin clearing away the debris, putting in work they weren't expecting to do in an effort to clean up, clear out, and re-establish things.

What a metaphor for life.

Life, unfortunately, isn't fair. It's not predictable, and it doesn't always make sense. Sometimes bad things happen. Sometimes it's a wrong place, wrong time thing. Sometimes it's a senseless tragedy. Sometimes it's the result of a preventable mistake or a lapse in judgment. Sometimes it's simply the Universe's roll of the dice. Sometimes the bad things are widespread like a pandemic, war, economic unrest, and hurricanes. Sometimes the bad thing happens only to us—an injury, a job lost, a pet dying.

Sometimes those bad things leave wounds that don't heal (technically labeled as Post-traumatic Stress Disorder), but oftentimes, those wounds do heal, leaving behind scars that remind us of what we've been through. And sometimes that healing process is the impetus for tremendous growth and positive change, driving us to be better than we originally were.

Wesley is the epitome of what we call post-traumatic growth in psychology and a real-life illustration of the Hero's Journey.

THE HERO'S JOURNEY

In every good story, the hero experiences difficult circumstances that must be overcome or faces an ordeal that shapes them into who they were meant to be. Superman's home planet was destroyed. Harry Potter was orphaned then raised by his less than stellar aunt and uncle. Katniss Everdeen faced death to save her sister before going on to become the heroine.

There is a struggle that leads to growth and strength.

Every single one of us is the hero of our own journey, and every single one of us will face adversity at some point, whether that's a traumatic event, a life-altering diagnosis, or a challenging situation. We will, inevitably, encounter something that knocks us down, takes a toll, and leaves behind some damage. What we do in the aftermath can define our future.

IT'S ALL ABOUT PERSPECTIVE

As you know, one of the hardest times in my life was when my vision loss worsened to the point that I could no longer drive. I was overwhelmed with sadness and fear. I truly believed that I was facing a bleak future, destined to be miserable and limited by my disability.

In hindsight, I feel for Past Ashley. I remember her despair. But I can also see how that dark time was the impetus for growth and change. If only I had known then that I was going to be okay. Better than okay, actually. That I was going to thrive. How much heartache could I have avoided if I'd known what lay ahead?

I often think about zooming in and zooming out. In the heat of the moment, we're completely zoomed in. There is nothing else. There was the Before and there is the Now, which we do not want.

What if we could zoom out and take in the entire timeline of our lives? It is quite possible that with a wider view, one in which we can see a longer trajectory, we may just realize that this Big Bad is actually the catalyst for something important. For some, it's a wake-up call that leads to key shifts in priorities, choices, or habits. For others, like Wesley, it is what propels them toward purpose.

How often, in retrospect, do we realize that difficult experiences were actually blessings in disguise? The heartbreak from being cheated on leads to leaving a lackluster relationship and finding real connection. Being laid off forces a career change, stress and insecurity morphing into re-energized passion. We just need to trust that we can weather the storm and have hope that what is so unwanted and hard today may be the seed of something beautiful down the road.

DON'T RUSH THE SILVER LININGS

Being in the eye of the storm can feel devastating. Something bad *is* happening. You may not have asked for it or caused it. It may genuinely feel like your world is falling apart. But in those dark moments, it is important to know that there is a path forward, a path toward a promising future, one in which you are happy.

I want to be clear, though. Post-traumatic growth does not mean being cheery, optimistic, or grateful about what is happening to you... at least not immediately. You have to go through the "ick" first. Yes, hold on to the hope that you will eventually find the silver lining, but you don't have to rush that. You might need a moment to wallow, and you definitely need to feel your feelings. Burying them backfires. The struggle is necessary. There is a beauty in the pain that will become evident over time.

ONE MORE NOTE ON PERSPECTIVE

There is a caveat to embracing the pain... and that's when the source of our suffering is our minds. Sometimes in our modern lives, we feel like something is a catastrophe that, if we're being real, just isn't.

I'm not a big fan of comparing pain. Someone always has it worse than you and that fact doesn't negate what you're going through. That said, I do believe that being real—acknowledging reality as it actually is—is critical. Our minds can blow things out of proportion so easily, amplifying our pain in ways that just aren't necessary.

A flight being delayed sucks, but we still get to fly. Through the air! Making it possible to travel anywhere in the world in a fraction of the time it used to take. Not getting Taylor Swift tickets is a disappointment, not a disaster. Someone being upset with you is uncomfortable, not earth-shattering.

So, when you find yourself caught in one of life's storms, ask yourself, "On the scale of bad things, is this a paper cut or a nuclear disaster?" Then, treat it accordingly.

If you're in a period of life that feels like rainbows and puppy dogs, enjoy it. Savor the moments because they will pass quickly. And if you're in the midst of a storm, know that, as Little Orphan Annie sings, "The sun will come out tomorrow."

"Sunshine all the time makes a desert."
—ARAB PROVERB

The Way I See It

Buck Up, Buttercup: You Can Do Hard Things

No one said life is easy and to pretend otherwise just doesn't make sense. We're going to be faced with hard choices and hard circumstances. Constantly. The way I see it, we can step back, take the path of least resistance, and passively let life happen to us. We can idly complain about the way things turn out, forgoing our agency and power and letting ourselves fall victim to whatever life throws at us. Or… we can take ownership, making active choices that craft our lives to be what we want them.

As much as I wish it were possible, we do not get to choose every aspect of our life circumstances. Some people hit the genetic lottery, and some of us don't. Some people are born with more privilege than others. World events impact us, through no fault of our own. Bad things happen.

Yet, we are not fragile. Like a palm tree bowing over in the face of a hurricane only to rise again afterwards, we can do the same. We are capable of enduring so much more than we know, of doing so much more than we believe is possible, if only we are willing. When you fail—and you will—and when you fall—and you'll do that, too—are you going to get back up and keep going, or are you going to give up and stay down?

It's not always about just sucking it up, grinning and bearing it, though. It's about knowing that you are strong and brave and doing the hard things that actually serve you. It's also about knowing when just barreling forward isn't doing you any favors. It's being honest and real with yourself. It's making the tough choices, doing what needs to be done to live the kind of life you want.

Life *is* hard. You *can* do hard things.

CHOOSE YOUR HARD

It shouldn't be this hard.

I just want it to be easy.

I need a break.

Between my job as a psychologist, networking with other professionals, and just because I'm chatty, I meet a lot of people. People with different backgrounds, life situations, and pain points. Yet, I hear that sentiment frequently.

We're tired. Tired of the struggle. Tired of feeling certain ways. Tired of working hard. And we just want it to be smooth sailing. How incredibly understandable is that? Especially when we consider what being on the brink of (or deep into) burnout feels like. We *do* get exhausted or overwhelmed or maxed out and just need some breathing room. That's a very real need.

At the same time, there seems to be this pervasive core belief that it is possible—and desirable—to be problem-free. It's understandable that we would hold this belief. After all, our minds are designed to solve problems and are quite capable of doing so. Take that natural tendency and then factor in societal messages that *if you just solve this one problem, you'll be happy*, whether that's getting that new thing you just have to have, an appearance issue, a relationship problem, you name it, and it's no wonder that we see problems as bad and constantly strive to get rid of them. Fix this one last thing, and voila, life will be easy. No more problems. It's Easy Street from here on out.

But that's B.S. and you know it.

THERE'S NO SUCH THING AS PROBLEM-FREE

Life is hard. It's solving one problem after another... and that's not necessarily a bad thing. While the promise of getting to a problem-free point is alluring, I don't think it's possible. Solving one problem creates another. If I solve the problem of needing money by becoming independently wealthy, I'd no longer have financial problems. Sure, but new ones may arise, like higher tax brackets or people using me for money.

If I solve the problem of dissatisfaction in a relationship, job, or location by moving on, don't I create the problem of uncertainty, starting over, or figuring out all the logistics?

If we go to the extreme and I solve the problem of removing every demand for my time and every stressor in my life, might that be replaced with the problem of boredom or purposelessness?

Even on a biological level, if I solve the problem of hunger or thirst, I'm creating the problem of needing to use the bathroom in the very near future.

So, if solving one problem will create another, then we're unlikely to get to the point of being completely problem-free, at least in a sustainable way.

Having realistic and helpful beliefs about problems is important. Perhaps problems aren't necessarily bad. Perhaps they can be reframed as challenges or even opportunities. And perhaps we can embrace or even welcome the idea that life is a series of problems to solve.

RADICAL RESPONSIBILITY

Radical responsibility as a concept holds that you are 100% responsible for 100% of the situations you find yourself in. It's not about fault or blame. Those are backward looking things. Radical responsibility is about acknowledging the situation you are currently in, regardless of how or why you got there, and taking ownership of your next step.

Think of it as: *What response am I able to take?* Response + able. Responsible.

What if we applied this radical responsibility mentality to this idea that life is a series of problems? What if we started asking ourselves what problems we want to solve? What if we started actively *choosing* our problems, at least when and where we can?

CHOOSE YOUR HARD

In my clinical practice, I tell my patients, "Once is a fluke. Twice is a coincidence. Three times is a pattern." Well, as embarrassing as it may be to admit, I'm well on my way to acknowledging a pattern of getting life-changing, perspective-shifting advice from Facebook memes. First, it was: *Just because life gives you a cactus, doesn't mean you have to sit on it.* I have said that countless times to my patients, to my friends, and to myself over the years. Now, it's: *Choose your hard.*

Choose your hard.

Meditating every day. Hard. Having a busy, racing mind. Hard. Your choice.

Working out. Hard. Dealing with poor health. Hard. Your choice.

Having a difficult conversation or being vulnerable. Hard. And hard. Having unhealthy relationships, lacking intimacy, being treated poorly. All hard. Your choice.

Learning new material that makes your mind stretch. Hard. Losing cognitive abilities. Hard. Yep, still your choice.

See what I mean? Hard now or hard later, which will turn into Now very quickly. Solve one problem, create another. Life is all about choosing the problems you want to solve, choosing your hard.

(Disclaimer: Yes, I absolutely realize that sometimes problems happen that we did not choose and had zero control over. We don't actually get to choose every aspect of our daily experience, but refer back to that first life-changing meme. We can sit on the cactus. Hard. Or we can do the work to take radical responsibility and take charge of our suffering. Hard. Your choice.)

"What pain do you want in your life? What are you willing to struggle for?"

—MARK MANSON

THE COST OF CONSTANT COMFORT

I n our modern lives, we spend our time moving from one comfortably curated experience to the next. Central heat and air allow us to maintain an optimal temperature regardless of the season. Readily available food allows us to eat whatever we want whenever we want. Instant streaming, two-day delivery, and Google mean that we are never without, at least not for long. Trigger warnings, denial, masking, and filters mean that we can operate in carefully crafted social and emotional circumstances. Factor in an underlying cultural myth that we can—*and should*— be happy all the time, and it's no wonder that so many of us have a warped relationship with discomfort. That is, we tend to see being uncomfortable as a bad thing to be avoided, something that shouldn't be happening, or something that shouldn't be a part of life.

And that attitude is incredibly limiting, if not downright harmful.

Sure, being comfortable—physically, emotionally, psychologically, socially—is preferable... or is it?

THE DOWNSIDE OF COMFORT

While being comfortable may signal that our needs are being met (for example, feeling well-rested is more comfortable to me than being exhausted, and we all know that adequate sleep is good for human beings), and being comfortable may reduce some stress (perhaps there is less need to worry about finances when you are financially comfortable), I believe that comfort is overrated. Here's why.

The more we get used to and expect to always be comfortable, the smaller our comfort zones become. In turn, we are more easily thrown for a loop when there is deviation in our experiences. Moreover, unwillingness to experience discomfort can come with dramatic ill effects.

Look at the lengths you go to in order to maintain comfort in any area of your life. Do you grab unhealthy food to avoid the discomfort of hunger as well as the discomfort that comes with having to prepare a nutritious meal or ride out a craving? Do you avoid the discomfort of physical exertion that comes with exercise?

What do you do to avoid psychological, emotional, and social discomfort? Do you numb out in unhealthy or unhelpful ways? Do you avoid asking the hard questions or having those tough conversations? How does that avoidance impact your relationships? Do you avoid doing things that make you feel awkward, insecure, or uncertain? To what end?

Like trying to shove a beach ball underwater, trying to avoid or get rid of uncomfortable feelings simply doesn't work long term. In fact, many of the measures we take to bottle up, shove down, suppress, or get rid of those uncomfortable feelings can actually intensify them or cause even bigger problems down the road. For example, eating your feelings can lead to more shame, disgust, and anxiety (and more eating of said feelings) while also creating health issues for your Future Self. Other consumption habits like shopping and mindless scrolling may help you avoid the discomfort of boredom or being alone with your thoughts, but they come with literal and figurative costs. Not taking chances may help you avoid the pain of failure or the discomfort of uncertainty... while also *causing* the pain of missed opportunities and regret.

Get this, there's even some fascinating emerging research that suggests that states of physiological discomfort like being hungry or cold can actually trigger a beneficial response on a genetic level, slowing the aging process. Our bodies were *designed* for periods of discomfort. It may actually be good for us!

THE SOLUTION

All of this to say, the pursuit of constant comfort can cause some unintended problems. The solution, I believe, is to get comfortable with being uncomfortable. Stepping outside your comfort zone in whatever capacity—socially, psychologically, emotionally, physically—can lead to growth and expansion. The bigger your comfort zone, the fewer things knock you off kilter. Your ability to sit with the "ick" without doing anything to make it worse in the long run (what psychologists call distress tolerance) can have a big impact on your life experience. Pushing into the discomfort strengthens us.

Moreover, reframing discomfort as a good thing to be sought out periodically can fundamentally change your relationship with it. It's comparable to the fitness enthusiast who has learned to view sore, painful muscles after a hard workout as a good thing, a sign of increasing strength, as opposed to seeing the pain as bad. Understanding how discomfort can lead to positive changes—and having the psychological strength to weather discomfort skillfully—can be powerful.

The things we do—or don't do—all in the name of staying constantly comfortable can cost us big time. So go, be uncomfortable!

"Be not afraid of discomfort. If you can't put yourself in a situation where you are uncomfortable, then you will never grow. You will never change. You'll never learn."

—JASON REYNOLDS

IT'S TIME TO STOP MAKING EXCUSES

I went to watch a small local production of *Rock of Ages*. A friend of a friend was in the show, and a big group went to support her. The plan afterwards was to go karaoke in honor of the performer's birthday. While I generally love any excuse to have a mic in my hand, it was nearly 11 p.m., and I found the prospect of a good night's sleep and a fresh mind for today much more appealing.

I didn't think twice about deciding to bail. While I knew a lot of the people in attendance, we're not really friends. We end up at some of the same events because of our mutual friend Kayla, but I did not feel any sense of obligation to stay out.

When I told Kayla I was going to head home, she surprised me by saying she was, too. The performer is a close friend of hers, so I assumed she'd be attending all of the birthday celebrations. Turns out, she wasn't feeling karaoke or a late night, either. As she said her goodbyes, I watched several of her friends try to persuade her to stay for the festivities.

Then, she did a glorious thing. She said simply, "I don't want to."

I think her directness may have surprised a few people, but I loved it so much that I commented out loud how much I appreciated her frank honesty.

WHY DO WE FEEL COMPELLED TO MAKE EXCUSES?

Where did our excuse-making culture come from? Why do we feel guilty for expressing ourselves, for being honest with ourselves and others? Why is it not enough to say no simply because we want to?

Somewhere along the way, someone decided that the only acceptable response to a request from someone else is a yes. If you're not going to say yes, then by golly, you better have a good, convincing reason not to.

Cue the excuses.

It also means that if someone doesn't offer an enthusiastic yes to *your* request, then you must be hurt or offended... unless, again, they have a solid reason—aka, excuse.

Oxford defines an excuse as "a reason or explanation put forward to defend or justify a fault or offense."

When did saying no become an offense? A fault? It's not! Yet, everyone seems to be operating from the same unspoken agreement that we're not allowed to say no or refuse requests unless we have a reason that absolves us of blame.

EXCUSES AREN'T ACTUALLY HELPFUL

Here's the kicker... do you know what actually happens when we offer excuses? When someone extends an invitation and we make an excuse to decline, what they really hear is, "I'd love to, but there's this obstacle in my way. If only that obstacle were removed."

What do they do? Like a good human, they try to be helpful! They offer solutions to help remove said barrier. Then, what happens for you? You experience them as pushy. And what happens next time? You come armed with the big gun excuses. Or you acquiesce and then spend so much energy dreading the future, plotting further excuses to get out of it and flaking at the last minute, or doing something you don't actually want to be doing. And the cycle continues.

Instead, if you kindly, but directly, said, "I appreciate the invitation, but I'm going to decline," your position is much clearer. Sure, they may press initially—"Why?" And you can give an honest explanation:

* "I don't want to."

* "I'd rather spend my morning at home."

* "Sleep is a priority to me, and I'm unwilling to compromise my health in that way."

* "It's not of interest to me."

* "I'd rather spend my money (or time or energy) on something else."

Or any variation of a clear but kind "thanks, but no thanks."

There is no longer a barrier that you must be rescued from. There is no resentment on your part for being roped into something you don't want to be doing. Your relationship is stronger because everyone involved knows that each person can and will take care of their own needs. It's a win-win-win.

Wouldn't that be amazing?

A NO ISN'T NECESSARILY PERSONAL

This excuse-free world is a two-way street. Not only do we have to muster the courage to be honest with others, we have to do a little deprogramming on ourselves. We must work to remember that a no is not a personal rejection. Someone else not wanting to do something you want them to does not have to mean anything other than you have different agendas or needs at the moment. It doesn't have to be an insult. It doesn't have to be a commentary on how they feel about you. It doesn't have to mean they are selfish or that you are out of line or whatever other super helpful interpretation your mind wants to throw out there.

A no is not a bad thing. Rather, I'd argue it's a good thing because, again, no one involved is resentful. No one is doing things out of obligation. And no one has to be codependent, taking on responsibility for others' emotions and experiences.

BE HONEST WITH YOURSELF

This plea for direct, honest communication applies to us as individuals as well. How often do we make excuses to ourselves?

EXCUSE: I can't catch up on my paperwork because I have to go to the doctor.
REALITY: I could do my paperwork in the waiting room—there's an app for that. I just don't want to.

EXCUSE: He doesn't mean to treat me that way. He can't help it.
REALITY: He's emotionally unavailable, but I'd rather lie to myself than be alone.

EXCUSE: I can't travel because I have kids.
REALITY: I want to be the kind of person who likes to travel, but I'm not. I'd rather spend my time and money on other things.

If we cut out excuses and are brutally honest with ourselves, we'd have to confront the fact that we're unwilling to do things we feel obligated to do or think we should do, which is absolutely okay. Sometimes the real work is on self-acceptance. Embrace who you really are and stop trying to be the person you think you *should* be.

Of course, if we're honest with ourselves, we may also realize that we don't like the reflection in the mirror. I like seeing myself as someone who is driven or spontaneous or friendly or whatever, but am I? Do my actions truly reflect that, or am I making excuses to preserve my ego and prevent myself from having to do the hard work of becoming the kind of person I want to be?

It's time to stop making excuses.

I often dream of a world in which everyone says what they mean and means what they say. One in which we do not shy away from hard conversations, one in which we are all clear but kind, one in which we are honest with ourselves and others. A world without excuses.

"If you really want to do something, you'll find a way. If you don't, you'll find an excuse."

—JIM ROHN

SIX LIFE LESSONS FROM MY FIRST 10K

I am not a runner.

At least that's what I've always told myself.

Sure, I've been curious about it at times, like when my friend April started running half-marathons in graduate school. She has this inspiring way of making crazy things—like halfs and sky diving—sound like experiences I need to have. I started to toy with the idea that running could be great... then, quickly gave it up once I actually tried it out. That was definitely something that was better in theory than reality.

In the million years since then, I've dabbled a bit, mostly intervals on a treadmill during which I'd glare at the timer the entire time, willing it to move faster. I think, at most, I got up to two miles, but still no love of running. It was a means to an end, just a convenient way to exercise. People told me that they preferred running outside to a treadmill, but not me. The one time I tried, I could've sworn I was at it for an hour. Turns out, it was actually only 10 (excruciating) minutes, no exaggeration.

But... for some reason, I decided I was going to run a 10K. You know what? I'm glad I did because I got a lot more than I anticipated out of this journey. I learned six important life lessons about success.

LIFE LESSON 1: SET A SMART GOAL.

As a psychologist, I know what that means: set Specific, Measurable, Achievable, Relevant, Time-bound goals. I help people do that all the time. Do I do it myself? Not so much. I get lax about it. This 10K was a nice reminder that SMART goals really are the way to go if you want to be successful. I signed up for the race months in advance as a commitment device to help hold me to a timeframe and keep me from backing out later. Then, I got specific about my goal: I was going to run the entire 10K on September 9. This goal seemed doable, but it would definitely take some serious training if I wanted any chance of succeeding.

Lesson: Your chances of success increase when you set SMART goals. Get clear and get specific!

LIFE LESSON 2: DON'T FALL FOR SNEAKY EXCUSES.

My significant other at the time was a runner and a morning person. I am neither. Still, I thought that running together might help in the motivation department. The night before our first planned run, he informed me that we'd have to get up around 6 a.m., maybe 6:15, to get it in before he had to go to work. "Okay, but that's going to be hard. I suck at getting up in the morning," I told him (at least a dozen times) in preparation for my inevitable grumpiness.

"You've already given up," was his gentle reprove from the other room. What was that? I expected assurances that it wouldn't be that bad, so his response caught me off guard… and he was absolutely right.

I tell my patients all the time that brains are liars and awesome rationalizers. Excuses can be insidious and convincing, but dang! I didn't even *realize* that I was already making excuses for falling short of my goal. It's like I was unknowingly setting the stage to fail.

After that lightbulb went off in my mind, I smiled, kissed his cheek, mentally thanked him for that lesson and resolved to get up at ridiculous o'clock… which I did. Thankfully, our run was rained out.

Lesson: Beware of excuses, justifications, and rationalizations. If you even slightly open the door for them, they'll come bursting through.

LIFE LESSON 3: SET PERSONAL RULES AND USE THEM TO YOUR ADVANTAGE.

It became apparent pretty quickly that I was going to need a formal training plan if I wanted to reach my goal. Willy-nilly going for a run here and there was not going to cut it, so I decided to use an app for guidance.

The early runs were super easy. We're talking 90 seconds of jogging. Piece of cake! As the times increased, though, so did the difficulty. I found myself struggling to complete the assigned runs, prematurely calling it quits more frequently than I'd like, so I started to question my formula. There had to be more to this than just logging the miles. Sure, stamina and endurance play a role, but I've seen an 80-year-old marathoner and people who don't look like runners doing similar distances. What, then, was the key? I figured it must be about mindset. All of a sudden, this 10K thing became more about hacking my mindset than training my body… and that realization made this challenge right up my alley.

Building on lesson number 2, I started paying attention. I recognized that as soon as thoughts like *Ugh! This is hard. I can't do this. How much longer? This is awful!* started springing up, it was usually a matter of minutes before I was walking. It made sense, though; thoughts drive behaviors. Running was strenuous enough for me, and those thoughts were the psychic equivalent of running with heavy weights on my ankles. How could I take my not-so-helpful mind out of the equation?

I decided to try out Personal Rules—premade decisions that you stick to without question. This strategy worked well for me when I tried the Whole 30, a 30-day restrictive clean eating plan… even at a networking event at a local brewery with tasty free off-limits beer and food. I closed the mental door on temptation by not even indulging a thought about *maybe just one…*

Turns out this strategy worked well with race training, too. I made the Personal Rule that *I run until the app tells me to stop.* No questions asked. No checking the time. No complaining in my mind. I didn't even entertain the possibility of breaking that rule. To help, I gave my mind the task of focusing on a super awesome audiobook instead. (*The Way of Kings* is fantastic!)

Lesson: Make decisions ahead of time and set them in stone. Don't even BEGIN to go down the mental path of questioning them. If you start to negotiate with yourself, you will lose. It's only a matter of time.

LIFE LESSON 4: IT'S OKAY TO TAKE A STEP BACK, REASSESS THE SITUATION, AND ADJUST ACCORDINGLY.

I felt like I had a breakthrough! I had cracked the mindset code. Granted, my Personal Rule approach didn't pan out every single time (I definitely broke my PR the day it was so hot I thought I was going to vomit and pass out), but I was able to shut down those mental ankle weight thoughts and, instead, focus on my audiobook and putting one foot in front of the other. My confidence grew, and this goal seemed realistic.

And then I got, what I can only assume, was the Bubonic Plague two weeks before the race. Not ideal. I had worked my way up to four miles running, and I knew I had a ways to go. My body, however, had other plans and refused to stop coughing and generally being gross.

Friends assured me that walking part of the race would still be a victory. Nope. I wanted to run the whole thing, and walking would be a failure. As the plague raged on, however, I became increasingly accepting of that idea. I wouldn't be able to *run* the whole thing, but at least I'd do it.

Lesson: Chase big goals but know that sometimes goals have to be reworked. Making adjustments based on new information or developments is not a failure. It's flexibility.

LIFE LESSON 5: SHOW UP. EVEN WHEN YOU DON'T WANT TO.

Sleep escaped me the night before the race. When that alarm went off before the crack of dawn (what is it with runners and the wee hours of the morning?), I was coughing. And *SOOOOOO* tired. Should I even go if I'm not going to be able to run without losing a lung? What's the point? Is it even in my interest health-wise to try?

I groggily googled coughing and running, which answered with a resounding *no*. I'm off the hook! Deal! I climbed back into bed, where I proceeded to toss and turn, mentally wrestling with myself. Am I just making an excuse? I learned that lesson already, didn't I? But no. Dr. Google says don't run with a cough. After 20 minutes of increasing guilt and disappointment, I got real with myself. I *was* making an excuse. I was just tired and didn't feel like getting up yet.

Fine. I got out of bed, put my tennis shoes on, shoved some peanut butter in my mouth, and called an Uber. I noticed that I already felt better. Deep down, I knew that going was the right decision, and I knew I wouldn't regret going even if I walked the whole thing.

Lesson: You miss 100% of the shots you don't take, right? Isn't giving up without even trying an even bigger way to fail than falling short?

LIFE LESSON 6: WHAT YOU PERCEIVE AS A LIMITATION MAY ACTUALLY BE THE KEY TO YOUR SUCCESS.

As I lined up with thousands of other runners, I focused on what a beautiful day it was. I could not have asked for better weather if I'd designed the day myself. There was absolutely no way I'd be able to run the whole thing, but at least I'd get some movement, and I'd enjoy being outside and listening to my book.

Despite knowing that running wasn't physically possible, I figured what the heck? I decided to give it a try—albeit an incredibly slow try—just to see what would happen. I'd made peace with the idea that I'd be walking the majority of the mileage, so there was no pressure to push my body beyond what it could handle. To my surprise and delight, though, it could handle a lot more than I thought. A mile passed almost without effort. No coughing. (And, honestly, no sweating or real exertion, either. I was pretty much running in slow motion.) I could keep going.

I hit the three-mile mark with ease.... and the realization that I WAS DOING THIS. And, what's more? That I could KEEP doing this. I was going to run a freakin' 10K!

Now, I've done a lot of work with self-limiting beliefs—working to change my own as well as to help my patients change theirs—and I thought I had a pretty good handle on them. As I ran, though, I contemplated just how thoroughly, unquestioningly sure I had been that I would not be able to run this morning... and just how wrong I was. I came dangerously close to not even trying, and it was a psychological slap in the face how off my predictive powers were. Not only was I going to cross the finish line despite being sick, I realized that I was going to be successful *because* I was sick. It forced me to start slow and stick with a sustainable pace. If I had been well, there's a pretty solid chance I would've started out much faster, burned out after a few miles, and struggled through the second half. I don't know if I would have made my goal or not, but I seriously doubt I would have enjoyed the experience as much as I did.

Lesson: Sometimes, the very thing you think will hold you back will actually hold the key to your success.

EPILOGUE

As I reflect on my first 10K, I feel proud. I accomplished something I wasn't sure I could do, and I learned a few important lessons along the way.

Imagine the shock when I found myself eagerly looking forward to my first post-race run... for no reason other than sheer enjoyment. The horror! I'm not a runner... *or am I?*

Bonus Lesson: With dedication and a mindset shift, that thing you dread may just turn into that thing you look forward to.

"That's what running does to lives... It's about the slow and painful process of being the best you can be."

—MARTIN DUGARD

LIFE ISN'T FAIR: HOW I LEARNED TO ACCEPT IT AND LET GO

"Because I'm dad, and I said so!"

Pops dropped that argument A-bomb pretty regularly when I challenged rules or threw fits because I didn't like his answers. "That's not fair! Your reasons don't make sense!"

They didn't have to. He was my dad. I lived in his house. He was legally and financially (and in all ways) responsible for me. As much as I didn't always like it, what he said went.

I hated that response. It really *wasn't* fair! It infuriated my adolescent brain, and I railed against the injustice. (Okay, I wrote a poem about "my dad, the ogre" in my journal and sulked in my room.)

Fast forward to that day in graduate school when, after learning all about child development and behavior management, I called my dad to tell him he was right. Life isn't always fair, and he didn't owe me a justification. In fact, he did me a service by helping me learn to deal with perceived unfairness. He *still* likes to bring it up.

GETTING STUCK

In my psychology practice, I frequently work with kids who "get stuck." They meltdown and are unable to let it go when things are unfair, not right, or don't turn out the way they expect. These are not bad or spoiled kids. Most have an anxiety disorder, and their brains may work a bit differently. Their thinking gets very rigid at times, and their emotions take over. The real problem is that their expectations are set in concrete, and they have to work really hard to learn to be more cognitively flexible.

Here's how I explain it to them: "Imagine that you're walking down the street, heading to a place you really want to go. All of a sudden, you fall into a giant hole. You really have your heart set on getting to that place, which is ahead of you, so you keep walking in that direction, repeatedly running into the wall now in front of you. If you keep doing that, you are literally just banging your head against a wall. That's not getting you anywhere! And if you sit down and give up, you're just stuck in a hole. That's also not getting you anywhere. Sometimes you have to stop, take a look around, and figure out a new plan. Maybe if you look behind you, there's a ladder or a rope, some way to get out of the hole. You won't see it, though, if you're stuck."

I teach them how to think more flexibly: Is this a paper cut or a nuclear disaster? What's another way to look at the situation? What are your ACTUAL choices? (I'd like someone to walk up and hand me a million dollars, but that's not a realistic option. The choices in front of me are work to make money or don't work and have no money. Lamenting the fact that someone isn't giving me a fat stack of cash is a waste of time and energy.)

Kids with anxiety disorders aren't the only ones who have to work to get unstuck. Many adults (with or without anxiety) get stuck at different times and in different ways.

About five years ago, I found myself seated at a friend's poker table for a friendly game of Texas Hold 'Em. I know the basic rules of the game, but I'm no shark. The buy in was low, and I was fully prepared to part with my chips. Since I didn't know the conventions of betting—when you're supposed to fold or raise based on what's showing and what's in your hand—I figured it was more fun to play than fold, so I did... with something like a pocket 2 and 7 (which is, apparently, one of the worst hands to get). I won that hand, and my friend flipped! "YOU'RE NOT SUPPOSED TO PLAY THAT HAND! EVERYBODY KNOWS YOU FOLD WITH THAT HAND!" Well, good sir. I played the hand I was dealt, and I played it well.

WHY AREN'T THINGS FAIR?

During our last election season, I, like so many people, decided to get into a heated debate with someone who lives on the complete opposite side of the sociopolitical spectrum from me. I was initially very frustrated during our discussion about some polarizing issue and our very different views on appropriate solutions when, in response to one of my undoubtedly solid arguments, he made the comment, "The world doesn't owe you anything."

That was a pause moment for me. An opportunity to stop and really examine some of my deeply held beliefs and assumptions, the filters through which I view and interpret the world.

It turns out, I agree. The world *doesn't* owe you anything. There are, what I believe to be, some basic human rights: that we all deserve to be treated with respect and to have the same freedoms regardless of race, gender, sexuality, wealth, disability, attitude towards dogs, whatever. The opportunity cards we are dealt, though— when and where we're born, our parents, genes, socioeconomic status, etc.—are not guaranteed. Many people have more or fewer or better or worse opportunities than average simply by virtue of luck. There are some very real hardships and obstacles that some people have to face and overcome to reach the same starting point as others. It's not fair.

LEARNING TO LET GO

Life is not fair, and the world does not owe me anything. What an awful way to move through life… or is it? I began to chew on these ideas. What would happen if I let go of the expectation that life should be fair or easy? Would that change my attitude and emotions? My experiences? Would it drive different choices or lead to different behaviors? What I initially heard as disheartening became empowering. I am in charge of my life. I CAN make things different. I don't have to be a victim of circumstance or past experiences or an uncertain future. I can learn and grow and cultivate the experiences I want to have. I can challenge my own assumptions and those of others. *I can play my cards any way I want to.*

When I stopped driving, I was in a pretty dark place mentally. It felt like I was losing my independence. I was overwhelmed with the uncertainty of my situation. How bad will my vision get? Will I go blind? Will I be able to support myself? Handle day-to-day stuff like grocery shopping? Travel? Have a social life? Will people even want to be my friend? I won't lie. I spent a lot of time wallowing in fear, grief, and self-pity and watching Netflix to distract.

Then, along came a Facebook meme that changed my life. It said, "Life may give you a cactus, but you don't have to sit on it."

I was stuck. Life had given me a cactus, and I was definitely sitting on it. I wanted answers to unanswerable questions. I wanted 20/20 vision. I wanted to be happy. The first two weren't options on my table. Continuing to dwell on them wasn't doing anything for me.

Happiness, however, was a different story. I believed—and still do—that happiness is not entirely (or even mostly) dependent on external circumstances—what you have or don't have. I can't change my vision (at least not yet. Come on, retina researchers, work your magic!), but I have more power and control over my life experience than I realized. I have a pretty unique skill set thanks to my profession. It was high time I started acting like it.

I stopped banging my head against the wall and began to look around. You know what I started to find? Ways to be happy despite my disability. More and more things that I CAN do, that I CAN control.

I have come a long way in accepting my situation. Acceptance doesn't mean that I like it, that I agree with it, that I would choose it if I could. (Believe me, I'd rather have 20/20. I'm not in a place to genuinely say that I'm glad I have vision loss, but I do recognize that it's made me who I am. Maybe I'll get there, but not yet.) It does mean acknowledging the reality of the situation, including what aspects are and aren't under my control, and choosing to let go of the unhelpful stuff that either won't make any meaningful difference or will actually only bring me down.

WRAPPING IT UP

When you find yourself stuck in an unfair situation, pause, take a breath, and look around. What do you actually have control over? Your attitude. Your thought process. Your actions. Those underlying expectations. All of those are within your control... you just might not like it. *I shouldn't have to do the work to let it go. It's not fair!* You're right. It isn't. Now what?

Take responsibility for the things you can change. Stop blaming others. Accept the things you can't change and find a work-around. "There is no fair. Play the hand you were dealt to the best of your ability." Who knows, you might even win.

"There is no fair. Play the hand you were dealt to the best of your ability."

—NAVAL RAVIKANT in *Tribe of Mentors* by Tim Ferris

WILLPOWER IS OVERRATED

My job as a clinical psychologist comes with many perks—good coping skills, setting my own hours, witnessing others transform and blossom—but one of the true luxuries is that I get to hear the real deal inside scoop. People share with me the pain points they hide from everyone else... and that allows me to see just how very similar we truly are.

I hate to break it to you, but you're not special.

Whatever it is, I can pretty much guarantee that you're not the only one to struggle, to question, to doubt, to fear, or to fail. Whatever it is, I'm pretty sure it just makes you human.

"Why can't I just do it?" she tearfully asked me.

"Because willpower is overrated," I said.

If you've ever gotten frustrated with yourself for falling short of a goal or not being able to make the change you wanted, keep reading.

WHAT IS WILLPOWER?

Part of the issue with relying on willpower is that a lot of people don't actually have a good understanding of what it is, and that sets them up to fail. Merriam-Webster defines willpower as "the ability to control one's own actions, emotions, and urges." And Merriam-Webster is part of the problem.

Sidestepping the argument that we can't actually control our emotions or urges, only how we respond to them when they show up, this is a poor definition. It implies that if we have unwanted emotions or urges or if we don't have perfect behavioral control, then we lack willpower, which gets interpreted as a personal shortcoming.

Instead, let's go with Google Dictionary's version that holds that willpower is "control exerted to do something or restrain impulses." This is a much more accurate definition, and it starts to hint at why we can't rely on willpower.

WHY WILLPOWER IS OVERRATED

With a crestfallen face, she concluded, "I'm lazy and weak."

"No," I corrected. "You're human."

I went on to explain that willpower is our ability to suppress, override, or basically veto an urge or impulse. It's a limited resource that gets used up as the day progresses. Think of it like gas in the tank or money in the bank. When you use it, it's gone and must be replenished. Willpower is not a character strength. Sure, some people may have more of it, just like some cars have bigger gas tanks and some people have bigger bank accounts. And just like some cars take more gas and some people have more bills than others, some of us have more urges and impulses to veto throughout the day. So, running out of willpower and succumbing to an urge (for action or inaction) does not necessarily make you lazy or weak. It means that you're spent.

Think of all of the urges and impulses you have to say no to throughout your day. No, desire to stay in bed. I have to get up now. No, urge to yell at the kids, I have to keep my cool right now. No, I can't hang up this Zoom call or roll my eyes at my coworker or eat the gallon of ice cream or watch the entire season of that show or speed or interrupt or avoid that overwhelming task or delete my entire inbox or... Can you see just how many little (and big) demands are eating up your willpower bandwidth every day? Is it any wonder that there's not a lot of gas in the tank left for extra stuff, like changing a comforting habit or starting something that takes energy and effort?

WE SET OURSELVES UP TO FAIL

Because we tend to misunderstand how willpower works and to overestimate how much we can rely on it, we set ourselves up to fail. We lie to ourselves, albeit unintentionally. We promise ourselves *I'll do this* or *I won't do that*, and we drastically underestimate how much willpower it will take to override urges to the contrary and just how much of this finite resource our Future Selves will have left. Fortunately, there are some things you can do to preserve or extend your willpower.

BUILD YOUR WILLPOWER

Like so many things in the world of psychological strength, willpower can be developed with repeated practice. Now, if we really want to get into the weeds, I'm not actually 100% sure that we increase our willpower so much as use habit formation to our advantage, cutting down on the need to exert willpower. Stay with me here.

Saying no to urges and impulses, especially if you say no to the same one repeatedly, can help you build new habits and shape your identity, which are going to look, on the surface, like increased willpower. For example, if you continually resist the urge to avoid anxiety-provoking things, you build the habit of courage. Then, you can rely on this habit, rather than sheer willpower, when triggers arise. And if you see yourself as someone who is brave, it's going to be easier for you to make that courageous choice.

Use Personal Rules

I am a big fan of using Personal Rules to my advantage. These can cut down on unnecessary rumination and help you build that willpower muscle, so to speak. Personal Rules are just blanket statements regarding what you do or don't do. For example, I don't drink soda. It's been so long now that it's just become a habit, which means I don't have to exert any willpower to stick with that. In the beginning, however, it wasn't that easy. I was a dedicated Dr. Pepper-a-day kind of girl, so when I first gave up soda, it was tough. If I started to debate in my head, *Do I want that sweet nectar of the gods or not?* it took a lot more effort (willpower) to choose water instead. I figured out that if I short-circuited the internal debate by shutting it down with a quick *I don't drink soda, end of discussion*, it was a lot easier, and my success rate went way up.

Think about the things that you already do... once you go through a lot of internal debate, struggle, or procrastination. Try using that as fuel to set your own Personal Rules. Are you someone who deliberates over whether you should accept an invitation from a friend? Just commit then use the rule *I follow through with commitments* when your mind wants to talk you out of going. Similarly, do you dread going to the doctor but know that you'll end up keeping the appointment? Just set the rule *I don't avoid appointments* and shut down the mental debate as soon as it starts. Bottom line, the internal back-and-forth is a major zap on your willpower and, if you go down that mental path, you're likely to lose. Fortunately, you can choose not to go there. While that may cost a little willpower up front, it's much less than what it takes to reel it back in when you've gone way down the dread-and-debate rabbit hole.

Design Your Way to Success

Design your environment and/or your schedule to increase your chances of success without overly relying on willpower to get you there. For example, I don't keep cheese in my house. It calls to me from the kitchen, sometimes a soft whisper, "Eat me," sometimes a demanding shout, "I'm here!" And I almost always lose the moderation battle. (The last time I brought a wheel of brie home, it didn't survive one sitting... I was alone.) You can take my route and just not bring temptations into the house. It's an easier willpower ask to just skip that section at the grocery store than to override the call from the fridge all day long.

Get creative here. How might you design your daily experience to help you resist urges and impulses without having to rely on willpower to do so? Can you:

* Delete the time-suck apps from your phone?

* Commit to plans in advance so you're not deciding in the moment?

* Meal prep on Sundays so you have healthy easy options throughout the week ready to go?

* Plan to do the tasks that take energy and effort or the ones you dread early in the day when you have more willpower available?

* Minimize distractions to prevent urges from getting triggered in the first place (e.g., put your phone on do not disturb or turn off notifications)?

- Create a commitment device? This is something that essentially forces your Future Self to stick with a decision your Present Self is making.

- Keep all of the equipment needed for a task or activity together and easily accessible? For example, laying your art supplies out so you can more easily get started on that project, packing your gym bag and putting it in the passenger seat of the car, setting that book on your pillow so you can read a few minutes before bed?

Keep in mind the limits of willpower and try not to set yourself up to fail by relying on it too much. We're all human, though, and we will inevitably get swindled into thinking willpower alone will be enough. When that happens, please be kind to yourself, then find a new way forward.

"I bought a book on willpower, but I only got halfway through it."

—STEWART LEE BECK

DON'T LET FEAR OF REJECTION HOLD YOU BACK

G iving a TEDx talk was a long-time personal goal and one I got to cross off the bucket list. The experience was everything I'd hoped it would be, and I'm incredibly proud of the talk I gave.

I won't lie. I've really enjoyed having people cheer me on and tell me nice things about what I said and what I've been able to do. That kind of stuff can go straight to a girl's head! But, I also think it's important to be real, to pull back the curtain and talk about the parts that no one saw. I don't want to just share the success with you. I want you to know about the failures, too.

I collected a lot of rejections along the way to TEDx.

SUCCESS AFTER FAILURE

I submitted my first application for a TED talk in 2017. 2017! And I submitted at least eight more before being accepted. (Honestly, that might be an underestimation. I stopped counting.) I got some flat-out rejections, "We got a lot of stellar applicants. Unfortunately, you weren't one of them," and completely ghosted by others. Twice I made it to the second round of consideration, only to be cut. But finally, the stars aligned, and TEDxEdina said yes.

There's a part of me that feels a little insecure putting my failures and rejections out there, a little voice that whispers you'll think less of me, that my success is somehow diminished now. But I know that little voice will grow louder if I listen to it, if I give it credence, and I don't want that to happen. So, instead, I'm leaning on some of my values here—authenticity and courage. I'm reminding myself of my why. Mostly, though, I'm telling myself that I'm in good company.

* Michael Jordan, one of the greatest athletes of all time, didn't make his high school basketball team.

* *The Four Hour Work Week* by Tim Ferriss, a book that literally changed the way I do life, was turned down by 26 publishers before ending up on the *New York Times* Best Seller list for years.

* Speaking of publishers with regret, 12 of them rejected J.K. Rowling's *Harry Potter* and 30 said no to Stephen King's *Carrie*.

* Steven Spielberg was rejected by film school multiple times.

* Thomas Edison's teachers reportedly said he was too dumb for school.

* Jerry Seinfeld was booed off stage at his first stand-up.

Oprah, Walt Disney, Bill Gates, Lady Gaga. There is no shortage of stories of mega successful people racking up a collection of rejections and failures along the way.

GET SOME GRIT

What these stories all have in common is grit. According to Dr. Angela Duckworth, the grit guru in the psychology world, grit is "passion and perseverance for long-term goals." It's the ability to persist in the face of setbacks and to grind it out when you don't achieve immediate success.

Grit is a good thing to have.

But we can do a deep dive into grit another day. The other thing these stories all have in common is that the possibility of rejection did not stop them. And not even just the possibility, but the actuality of it. These people are all masters of collecting rejections.

COLLECTING REJECTIONS

I first came across this concept years ago in the context of my psychology practice. I was working with a socially anxious teenager who did some intensive treatment at a clinic out-of-state. When he returned to Kansas City, he shared that one of the most impactful things he learned was to collect rejections. He went on to explain that he had been convinced and encouraged to actively do things with the intent of getting rejected.

Keep in mind, he was supremely afraid of rejection, so much so that he had trouble talking to peers, making phone calls, and even functioning in everyday life. By actively trying to get rejected, though, he learned that he didn't actually get rejected nearly as often as he thought he would. His mind had lied to him. Frequently. Promising that if he did or said whatever, then others would reject, ridicule, or shun him.

Turns out, they didn't. And those experiences of proving his mind wrong shifted his fears.

In the course of trying to collect rejections, we get to realize that sometimes our fears are unfounded. If we're willing to take the risk, to put ourselves out there in relationships, professional settings, business endeavors, hobbies, whatever, we just might be pleasantly surprised by the outcome.

But sometimes, we actually do get rejected.

RECOVERING FROM REJECTION

No.

Those two little letters can strike a chord of fear. Yet, as with nearly everything we fear, it's not as bad as we anticipate and with repetition, we get desensitized to it. Sure, hearing a no, being turned down, or failing, whatever that looks like, isn't fun in the moment, but there's value in it.

Hearing no helped me develop thick skin. I was disappointed when I got my first rejection. The fourth? Not so much. It was easier to shrug off. I noted the disappointment but didn't let my mind spiral or ascribe a lot of meaning to it. And I chose to keep going, to trust that it would eventually happen. I reminded myself that I really had nothing to lose, other than some ego.

FAILURE CAN BE KEY TO SUCCESS

In hindsight, I am actually grateful for all those rejections. Maybe it's revisionist history, but I truly believe they were important. Necessary. Blessings in disguise. If my first application had been accepted, I would have been on cloud freaking nine...and I would have delivered a mediocre, forgettable talk.

The essence of my big idea was there, but the talk would've fallen flat. I believe that in my bones. I know what I knew then and what I was capable of at that time. The last few years have given me the life experiences, wisdom, courage, and skill to create and deliver a much better talk. I'm glad it was 2022 Ashley and not an earlier version who got to take the stage.

WATCH MY TEDX TALK

DON'T LET FEAR OF REJECTION HOLD YOU BACK

At this point in life, I love the mentality of collecting rejections, of viewing them as valuable pieces of corrective information, opportunities to build resilience and confidence, and stepping stones to something greater.

Embracing rejection is not a masochistic endeavor. It's a psychological strength one. It requires a fundamental shift in how you view rejection. Rather than labeling rejection as capital-B-Bad, we must recategorize it as a neutral, if not good, thing.

Think of FAIL as "First Attempt At Learning"

If babies weren't willing to fall hundreds of times, they'd never learn to walk. We'd all be scooting around on our bottoms. Naturally, we know that falling—*failing*—is part of the learning and growing process. Somewhere along the way, though, we're taught that it shouldn't be.

Realize that "no" doesn't mean anything about you as a person. It just means that particular door is not open to you right now. Try another. It makes me think of trying to find a place to eat dinner with April the other night. The Uber dropped us off at the restaurant that was recommended and that Google said was open. The door was locked. It's not like we gave up. No more dinner ever! We just changed direction and tried two more places until we found one that was open.

Trust Yourself

You may be disappointed, devastated even, but know that you are strong enough to handle it. You are not fragile, and you can do hard things.

Ask yourself, where are you letting the possibility of rejection or failure, the fear of hearing no hold you back? How much potential could you unlock if you were willing to collect rejections? How much freer would you feel if rejection rolled off your shoulders? What would you do or say? What risks would you take if you were willing to view rejection as a good thing?

"By the time I was fourteen the nail in my wall would no longer support the weight of the rejection slips impaled upon it. I replaced the nail with a spike and went on writing."

—STEPHEN KING

SLOW DOWN TO GO FARTHER, FASTER

"How am I going to get through this?" one insightful yet drastically overcommitted teen tearfully asked me during our therapy session. "It's too much."

Or was it the new mom? The working parent? The teacher? The doctor? The stressed out entrepreneur?

The answer for most seems to be *work harder, do more.* That's the only way to get it all done, and that's the only way to be successful.

But is it?

COUNTERINTUITIVE ADVICE

Over coffee this morning, I was reading a book on longevity, and the author, Dr. Peter Attia, made the case for slowing down to go faster. He was talking about it in the realm of exercise, and I can relate.

A couple months ago, my trainer, Emily, noticed that my left shoulder blade was doing this weird jutting out off-track thing during certain exercises. It wasn't painful. In fact, I couldn't even feel that it was happening. I was good with continuing full steam ahead.

She, on the other hand, immediately had me drop the amount of weight I was using and spend several weeks training some tiny, precise movements to correct the issue. I didn't feel like I was doing much, but I understood her point. If I keep pushing to lift heavier weight with my body out of whack, then one of two things will happen: 1) I'll plateau at a lower weight because my body's cheats will eventually not be able to compensate for poor mechanics, or 2) I'll end up injured. Or both. Neither is in line with what I really want.

She made me slow down so I could correct my form, which will eventually allow me to safely make more strength gains. Two trusted sources preaching slow down to go farther, faster when it comes to health. It's not just with exercise, though, that this advice holds.

FULL SPEED AHEAD GETS YOU STUCK

In the South, where I grew up, muddin' is a thing. It can be a blast to hop in a truck or on a four-wheeler and ride off-road through muddy terrain, but you have to know what to do when you get stuck. The urge can be to throttle the gas—harder is better, right? But that actually makes the tires just spin, digging you into a deeper hole. The real solution is to go slow. Being patient and methodical lets you get the traction you need to eventually move forward.

How about a more mundane example? When you're already late and you can't find your keys, it's natural to frantically start searching. You buzz around your home, tossing things out of the way as you try to find your keys. In your haste, you may haphazardly move from one location to another, repeating some and skipping others. Your mind is telling you that you must hurry, hurry, HURRY, but in doing so, you are actually taking longer to find those keys.

If you can pause and go slow, you just might give yourself a beat to remember where you last had your keys. And if you're still drawing a blank, you can at least search systematically. With a little bit of strategy, your mission is likely to be more successful.

MAKE IT A LIFESTYLE

Oftentimes, it's not a single frantic moment that's tripping us up... it's a *lifestyle* of frantic moments. If your day-to-day is razor-thin margins and exhausting multitasking, tinged with overwhelm, dread, or near-breaking-point irritability, you desperately need to slow down.

In business and in life, blindly charging forward with the work harder, do more mantra may backfire. You may find yourself in an unsustainable position, exceeding your capacity. Moreover, your efforts may be misguided, yielding suboptimal results if not actually creating more problems for Future You to clean up.

RECOGNIZE WHEN YOU'RE HITTING CAPACITY

Imagine a pint glass. You fill it with your liquid of choice. It nears the top, reaching its capacity. It cannot expand to hold more, yet you continue to pour. What happens?

It overflows and makes a giant mess.

Now imagine yourself as that glass. How often do you try to cram in too much?

Like it or not, you are not a boundless fountain of energy, time, attention, and drive. You are limited by your capacity. If you try to apply the work harder, do more philosophy when you're at (or past) your capacity, things are going to get messy.

Instead, slow down and figure out what you really need. Do you need a new system? Or do you need a new mindset?

IMPROVE YOUR SYSTEMS

Like my wonky shoulder blade, any crack in your systems—how you manage your time, your energy, your household, your job, your relationships—will widen and worsen when under pressure, ether capping your progress or resulting in injury. We must take the time to fill in the cracks and ensure a strong base before we add strain.

Consider the friction points in your day-to-day. Where are the systems breaking down, and how might you be able to strengthen them? Is dinner time always a mad dash to the store or a restaurant? What would happen if you dedicated a couple hours on the weekend to meal prepping? Yes, you have to spend more time up front, but the time, energy, and stress saved throughout the week may be a game changer. Slow down to go farther, faster.

Are mornings rough? What can you do the night before to make them smoother? How can you enlist help from others to change things up? Are you constantly doing repetitive tasks? Wouldn't slowing down to find ways to automate or increase efficiency make a difference for you in the long run?

More of the same will get you more of the same. It's not about working harder. It's about working differently... which brings us to mindset.

CHANGE YOUR MINDSET

Our beliefs act like instructions for how to operate in life. Unfortunately, some of them just don't do us any favors. In this context specifically, let's work on two common yet unhelpful ones.

Belief: Hard work is the answer.

As I've already touched on, work harder is the automatic solution that many people jump to... but it may not be working for you. Hard work is absolutely not a bad thing. *Misapplied* hard work, though, is a waste. If you are exerting increasing effort toward something that isn't effective or sustainable, you're going to spin your wheels or burn out. Plain and simple. Try on *work smarter, not harder.* See how that belief fits for you.

Belief: I don't have time.

That's another pesky belief that hinders more than it helps. Like with the mad dash search for keys, sometimes taking a few extra minutes saves you exponentially.

Your kid is whining. Instead of snapping at them to knock it off (which would be completely understandable—whining *is* hard to tolerate), it may behoove you to take two minutes to actually talk with them about what is going on and what they need. That investment of time builds your relationship, which will pay dividends in the future, and may lead to a successful resolution of the situation in less time (e.g., maybe what they really need is a snack, and a banana would prevent an afternoon of meltdowns for both of you).

Coming down with an illness or just feeling really run down? Taking the time to rest may restore your energy enough to let you be more efficient and effective later. And certainly taking five minutes to do whatever self-care task your mind is talking you out of (you have five minutes, I promise) may make a notable difference in your stress level, again, allowing you to do more in the long run.

THE PARADOX

In psychology, so many of our strategies hinge on doing the opposite of what comes naturally. In fact, we call it Opposite Action in one school of therapy, but it shows up all over the place.

If you want to overcome fear, face it instead of avoiding it. If you want to cool anger, speak softly instead of yelling. If you want to feel close to someone, share your shameful secrets instead of hiding them. If you want to have healthier relationships, say no or ask for what you need instead of being agreeable all the time. It's counterintuitive, but so many effective things are.

If you want to go farther, faster, slow down.

"Sometimes you need to slow down to go fast."

—JEFF OLSON

WHY YOUR REST ETHIC IS CRITICAL TO YOUR SUCCESS

I may regret broadcasting this... but I recognize that as what it is: fear of being judged and fear of letting my humanness show in a way that might undermine my professional credibility. I'm not a big fan of letting fear make my decisions, though, so here goes.

I had a friend in town from Saturday to Tuesday. Monday night, a "school" night, we stayed up until 2 a.m., wrapped up in winding conversation over an unnecessary extra glass (or two) of wine. This isn't a lifestyle choice I make very often these days, as I know how important sleep is, and I refuse to show up to professional commitments as less than my best if I can help it. Fortunately, I knew I didn't have anything until the afternoon, so I'd have time to sleep in.

Which is exactly what I did.

I woke up per usual, chatted with my friend for a bit before she hit the road, then I hit the sheets again. I got up a couple hours later to get ready for my day, feeling rested... and guilty.

Yep. Guilty.

As I talked to another friend, Amanda, later that night, she asked how my visit was. I told her a long-winded version of "lovely," but then explained that I was struggling with the decision to stay up late and sacrifice my morning. To this, my brilliant and empathic friend reminded me that life is measured in those kinds of moments—nights with a close friend, filled with laughter and connection. She was right, of course (one of the perks of having a therapist in your inner circle).

IT'S ALL ABOUT THE WORK ETHIC...UNFORTUNATELY

Like most of my fellow Americans, I was indoctrinated into the mindset that hard work is the path to success. A strong work ethic is one of your greatest assets. Any minute not consumed with productivity is wasted time. Those who don't work hard are lazy. Busy is a badge of honor.

And I pushed back on that. Hard.

Years ago, when I stumbled across the field known as Life Design, coinciding with turmoil in my life that had me questioning so many things, I began to redefine how I valued time. I subscribed (and still do) to the notion that time is the most non-renewable resource on the planet, and I began to get very intentional about how I spent mine.

Long story short, that led to a pretty fantastic work-life balance that had me, surprisingly, doing better financially than I ever had before with more discretionary time to spend on non-work activities.

Then a pandemic hit.

As everyone's mental health went down the drain, demands for psychological services skyrocketed. That, combined with other projects on my goal list, made it easy to let that hard-won balance slip.

While I still believe that time is precious and that productivity is not the be-all, end-all of your worth, my actions lately haven't necessarily reflected that. Hence the guilt for taking a morning to nap and indulge (care for?) myself.

I am sharing all of this with hopes that:

1. You can relate (and that you're not sitting there judging me).

2. We can keep each other accountable for letting wellbeing, not productivity or money, be the underlying deciding factor for how we spend our time.

3. I've adequately set the stage for what I really want to talk about: rest ethic.

WHAT IS REST ETHIC?

Months ago, a mentor and friend, Dr. Loren Conaway, suggested that I consider writing about rest ethic. It was something that had come up in her practice recently, and she thought it would be a topic that would resonate with others.

I think she's right.

I have to be honest, though, it wasn't a term I was really familiar with, so I just made note of it and tucked it away for later. I finally did a bit of a dive into the concept. Turns out, I'm fully on board with it!

Rest ethic has to do with how well you recharge, restore, and recover from your work efforts. It seems synonymous with self-care to me and is essential not only for sustainable wellbeing but also for peak performance.

WHY REST ETHIC MATTERS

Many people balk at the idea of rest. They believe that time not spent being productive is wasted and, therefore, feel guilty about it. They fear that they will lose progress or momentum. They don't feel like they deserve it or have done enough to earn it. Or they mistakenly believe they do not—or should not—need it.

The reality, though, is that rest is JUST AS IMPORTANT as work.

Like yin and yang, rest and work complement each other. They are two halves of a whole, integral to success and wellbeing. Like night balancing day, sleep balancing wakefulness, inhaling balancing exhaling, rest balances work.

If you want to build muscle strength, you must take time off between workouts. Serious lifters know that rest days are *just as important* as training days. If you want to find creative ways to solve a problem, you must step away from the problem. Creativity happens when our brains are relaxed or in a playful, positive state, not an anxious or stressed one. If you want a rich life, you need to invest in relationships, not just your salary or 401K.

We need to take our rest ethic as seriously as our work ethic and value them equally, as one without the other is going to lead to strife. I mean, no one lying on their deathbed laments, "If only I had worked harder..."

WHAT IS REAL REST?

Rest is not the same thing as sleep. Rest is a gathering of energy and resources, a refilling of the cup from which you've been pouring. I like to think of it as recovering whatever you've expended, whether that's physical energy, mental energy, emotional energy, or social energy.

Rest might mean exactly what you envision for a kindergartener: lying down and stilling your body and mind. Or it might mean switching gears from work to play, engaging different parts of your personality and cognitive faculties. It might mean checking out from real life and escaping into a novel or a daydream. It might mean watching a show or going down a YouTube rabbit hole (though watch out for those because, if we're being real with ourselves, they're not usually all that restorative).

Experiment with different kinds of activities or—pause for dramatic effect—the concept of just being. As in, not *doing* anything. See what recharges you. Then prioritize it.

NEXT STEPS

If you're still not on board with the whole idea of a rest ethic, then, by all means, stick with the productivity is king mindset... and recategorize restful activities as ALSO being productive. Because they are allowing you to recoup spent energy so that you can expend it all over again, frame rest as a necessary part of a highly productive lifestyle. Personally, I don't love that argument for a number of reasons, but, hey, whatever works!

The bottom line, find ways to build rest into your day and see what impact it has on your mind, body, and spirit. You just might find that as your rest ethic gets on point, your work improves, too. (And, yes, I will be taking my own advice on this one!)

"You were not just born to center your entire existence on work and labor. You were born to heal, to grow, to be of service to yourself and community, to practice, to experiment, to create, to have space, to dream, and to connect."

—TRICIA HERSEY

ARE YOU SELLING YOURSELF SHORT?

I am fascinated by people who seem to beat the odds. The ones who play life by their own rules, tackle big hairy audacious goals, the kind of people who are truly, fully living. It's easy to look at them and think, *I could never do that*. We chalk their success or good fortune up to luck or talent, or we conclude that we are somehow fundamentally different from them and, therefore, unable to grasp the same heights. I vehemently disagree with that conclusion, though. Instead, I believe that the more apt way to look at it is if it can be done, then why not by me?

WE SELL OURSELVES SHORT

We often sell ourselves short, buying the belief *I can't*. We take it as fact without recognizing the complexities of what's really happening. We can let our minds operate according to their default programming, play it small, and stay stuck... OR we can develop the psych strength we need to unlock our full potential and cultivate the life experience we want.

Think about the people you look up to with some degree of envy... followed by the sentiment *but I could never*. Maybe it's the person running a cool company or the parent who seems to actually enjoy their kids. Perhaps it's the person who has deep and loving relationships or the one who is maintaining positivity despite a difficult diagnosis. Maybe you admire the world traveler or the unflappable, always calm in a crisis friend. Maybe you aspire to heal from past trauma, forgive someone who wronged you, build a financial safety nest, be a homesteader, learn to play the drums. Whatever it is, if it can be done, again, why not by you?

IS IT A REAL CAN'T... OR A NOT YET?

Despite what you might be thinking right now, I am not a just-be-positive-you-can-do-anything-you-set-your-mind-to kind of person. I actually believe wholeheartedly that we must be real with ourselves. There are legitimate limitations that may preclude us from doing things that we see are possible for others. For example, I am not physically capable of reading street signs or seeing cars at any significant distance. Can I drive? Technically, yes. I know how to drive. Can I do so safely? Absolutely not. So, being a race car driver isn't in the cards for me.

Physical or legal limitations do exist, and we need to accept those and work within the bounds of reality. The issue is that so many people mistakenly identify things as limitations that aren't actually. They accept *I can't* as fact instead of recognizing it as an excuse, a bit of misinformation, or a willingness issue.

Yes, by all means, please do consider whether real, immutable variables will prevent you from reaching what you dare to desire. But do so with the knowledge that your mind, unless you put it in check, is going to miss the mark here. A lot.

Instead of *I can't...*, ask yourself, *how can I...?*

That question alone can put you on a different trajectory, one of growth toward success rather than resignation and mediocrity. But let's go deeper. Consider the people who have something that you want, who live life in a way that you admire, or have accomplished something that seems out of the realm of possibility for you. Then, consider these key questions.

What beliefs would I have to hold to accomplish that?

Beliefs are a driving force in how we approach and experience life. They can hold us back, limiting us in ways that we are often not even aware of, but it doesn't have to be that way.

You'll need to first understand that beliefs are things our minds take to be true, but that is not the same thing as capital-T-Truth. Beliefs are NOT facts. Even when they *feel* real, down to our bones, *beliefs are just mental creations*, not a reflection of an objective, unalterable reality. *Beliefs can be reworked.*

Look to the person who has done what you wish you could and think about what their belief system must be. Do they likely believe that anything less than perfect is a failure? Or do they believe that failing fast is the key to learning, growth, and success? Do they believe that they are unworthy? Or do they likely believe that they have inherent value? Do they, deep down, believe that hard things are bad and to be avoided? Or do they believe that they can do hard things and/or that hard things are worth doing?

Do some serious reflection here. My guess is that you and your role model are operating with a different set of assumptions—beliefs—about how the world works, what is possible, and why. Then, get to work adjusting your mindset.

What about identity?

Our identity is really just the collection of beliefs about who we are and what people like us can and can't do. Like all beliefs, those related to our identity are created by our minds. Sure, our identity is based on experiences and what we've been taught throughout life, but it is not set in stone any more than our beliefs about, say, politics or what kind of music is the best.

Deep down, are you a leader? Are you someone who can handle stress? Are you lovable? Are you risk averse? Are you the kind of person who trusts easily? The kind of person who compromises? Are you good at math? Music? Technology?

Can you see how your answers to those questions may influence what you believe is possible for you and, therefore, what decisions you make?

Our identity plays a huge role in how we live life. And for most of us, our identity is just subconscious programming that needs to be updated. And it can be. I am not the same person I was twenty years ago, thank goodness, and I doubt you are either. Our identities shift over time, and, fortunately, we can harness that to intentionally shape who we see ourselves as.

This is where a lot of people get stuck, though. They accept that they're just not the kind of person who can do whatever it is they envy. The reality, though, is that, barring a real non-negotiable limitation, they are probably quite capable of doing that very thing IF they can shift their identity AND they are willing to do the other necessary work, which brings us to...

What habits or behaviors would I need?

Habits and behaviors make more of a difference in terms of success than just about anything else. To illustrate, I want to write a novel. I know that it can be done because I read novels constantly. And I know it can be done by people who did not go to school for writing because I have two incredibly talented friends who have proven that. Heck, I even believe that I can do it—if it can be done, then why not by me, right?

And yet, I haven't. Why?

A novel won't write itself, and I think it's a misconception (a faulty belief, which I can change!) that you must wait until the mood and inspiration strike to sit down and furiously bang out the text. Instead, my author friends (and seasoned pros like Stephen King) have a habit of writing. They sit at their computers and write. Regularly. This is something that I can emulate and, in doing so, would start to craft my identity as a writer and move the needle on reaching my goal of writing my own novel.

And this can apply to anything.

What habits and behaviors do relationship masters have? How do they approach conflict? How do they maintain intimacy? Do you do it the same way? If not, how can you adopt their habits? What about the habits and behaviors of people who seem to have inner peace? Do they practice mindfulness? Set boundaries?

If you want the outcome someone else has gotten, look at what they do on a daily basis. We underestimate the power of small, consistent actions.

What knowledge, skills, or resources would I need and how/where can I get them?

There may be a huge gap between you and the person who is inspiring you. But knowledge, skills, and resources can be acquired... if you are willing to identify what you need, seek it out, and put in the work. You're not going to become a professional basketball player based on hopes and dreams. It's endless hours of technical practice and conditioning... just ask Michael Jordan. He did the work.

You're not going to become a millionaire through wishful thinking. Aside from winning the lottery or getting a big inheritance, you're going to have to figure out what knowledge and skills you need. Do you need financial literacy? Do you need business know-how to build your empire? Let's rope in the previous points here, too. What are your beliefs about money? Are they supporting you or holding you back here? What are your habits and behaviors related to money? Again, are they supporting your goal or hindering it? What do other millionaires believe or know to be true? How did they get to where they are? How can you follow in their footsteps?

Finally, ask yourself what would I have to give up in order to achieve what I want... and am I willing to do that?

If you really want to run a marathon, are you willing to give up your Saturday mornings to train? If you really want to be your own boss, are you willing to endure the uncertainty that comes with entrepreneurship? If you want to break free from anxiety, are you willing to learn what that takes and to practice it, even if it's scary or uncomfortable? If you want a cohesive group of friends, are you willing to put yourself out there to find and build those relationships? If you want to feel rested, are you willing to forgo the nighttime scrolling to be in bed at a decent hour? So often, we say, "I can't," when what we really mean is "I am unwilling."

The bottom line is that we can all do so much more than we think is possible, and our life experiences can be so different from what they are. It just takes intentionality and the work of shifting beliefs, reshaping our identities, and changing our habits. *None of that is easy, but it is all possible.* More than possible, even. If it can be done, then why not by you?

"If it can be done, why not by me?"

—DR. ASHLEY

DARE TO DO THE IMPOSSIBLE

Guess what... I learned how to drive a motorcycle this week!

This is a big deal. A really big deal... because I'm legally blind. I haven't been able to drive anything in years. So, you see, driving a motorcycle is a huge deal for me because it means doing the impossible.

I am not reckless, and I don't harbor any illusions about my limitations. I know that there are things that I am not physically capable of doing (like reading a street sign or regular font on a phone). It's not a matter of not believing in myself. It's a matter of my retinas not working properly.

That said, I am, however, willing to challenge what my brain tells me and to stretch well beyond my comfort zone. And that paid dividends.

Initially, I felt nervous and apprehensive. Afterwards, exhilarated and alive. And overwhelmed with emotion. It's hard to put into words how it felt to succeed at something I didn't even believe was possible. To feel brave and capable and independent. To feel free and unburdened by my disability, even if only temporarily. It was incredible.

I've had a chance to reflect on this powerful experience, to consider what it takes to dare to do the impossible. This is what I've come up with.

QUESTION WHAT IS POSSIBLE

In 2015, I made the decision to stop driving. It was glaringly clear that I was no longer able to safely drive a car, and I'm sure that stubborn refusal to accept that would've resulted in someone getting hurt. It was just a matter of time. Even transports like golf carts and bicycles get a little dicey unless I go exceptionally slow or have someone leading the way. So, I learned how to navigate the bus system and was incredibly grateful when Uber became a reliable option.

Since then, it's not like my vision has improved any. In fact, it's gotten worse. So, I've accepted as fact that driving a motorized vehicle is not an option for me, at least not until Tesla masters the self-driving car.

Driving an actual motorcycle by myself was not in the realm of possibility.

Then my dear friend Michael threw out the question, "Do you want to learn how to drive my motorcycle?"

My knee jerk reaction was, "I don't think I can."

Michael knows me well and is well-acquainted with my vision. He's also not reckless. I absolutely believe that he would not put me—or his bike—in a position to be harmed, so his question made me pause to consider... Could I?

Lesson: Too often, we accept our perceived limitations as fact when they may not be anything other than belief. Question what is actually possible and dare to dream that something just might be.

FIND THE RIGHT SUPPORT

With patient teaching and a lot of encouragement, I learned how to control the bike. If Michael hadn't believed so steadfastly in my capability, this experience would not have happened.

Now don't get me wrong. He was not unrealistic. This was not a Pollyanna-you-can-do-anything-you-set-your-mind-to-if-you-just-believe-in-yourself scenario here. He clearly told me not to go above second gear to keep the speed in a range my visual field could keep up with. He didn't turn me loose on a busy street where I'd be a liability to myself or others. He kept a firm grasp on meaningful parameters, but encouraged/pushed me to succeed well beyond what I thought was possible.

Lesson: You don't always need a social ankle weight tethering you down masquerading as a "voice of reason." You need people who help clear the path to allow you to succeed and people who see your strengths and potential and challenge you to push the boundaries, to be the best version of you that you can be.

SET YOURSELF UP FOR SUCCESS

Beyond those parameters of speed and location that kept me safe, we also did this at night. For many people, this may seem like an odd choice. For me, however, this was truly the condition that allowed me to be successful.

My vision is drastically affected by light, and my eyes basically shut down in brightness. If we'd tried this during the afternoon sun, there's no way I could've done it. Opting to try this venture in the dark, and in a neighborhood I was very familiar with, helped offset my visual limitations.

Lesson: Consider the context. Choose conditions that counteract your weaknesses, amplify your strengths, and set you up for success.

BE BRAVE

It takes courage to try something that you're not sure you can do. You have to be willing to risk failure and the pain that comes with it. When the outcome isn't guaranteed, when you're not 100% certain how things will turn out (and let's be real here, we never *truly* know how things are going to go), it can be uncomfortable at a minimum to outright terrifying to take the leap, depending on the perceived risk.

Being brave doesn't mean feeling confident, having certainty, or feeling calm. It means embracing the discomfort, not letting anxiety hold you back, and doing it anyways. Being brave is a strength that can be developed, a habit that can be cultivated. And it's invaluable.

Lesson: There's no way to stretch your comfort zone, reach your peak, or hit your actual ceiling without tapping into courage.

THE RIGHT MINDSET

I am continually awed by realizations of just how powerful beliefs can be. I don't think anything else shapes our life experience as much as our beliefs do. They impact literally every aspect of our life from the automatic thoughts and reactions we have in the moment to our sense of identity to the decisions we make to how we interpret what happens to us. The gravity of our beliefs is enormous. Yet, very few people have a good grasp of how beliefs work, how they are formed, and how to ensure that they are not exerting a negative impact on life. That's too bad.

With the right conditions and the right kind of support—sitting squarely atop the foundation of a strong belief system—you just may be able to exceed what you thought was possible. I certainly did. While I won't be racing in any Motorcycle Grand Prix or even investing in a bike of my own, that ride was a pivotal moment for me and one for which I will be eternally grateful.

"Nothing is impossible. The word itself says
I'm possible."

—AUDREY HEPBURN

The Way I See It

SECTION 6

Happiness Is Possible

I have been fascinated by the science of happiness since graduate school when I designed my master's thesis around the topic. My study became more urgent and personal as I came to grips with vision loss in the After. Through consuming research and philosophy and my own blind stumblings, experiments, experiences, and luck, I've learned a few things about the nature of happiness.

We all want it, yet it can be so very elusive. In part, because we misunderstand it. We believe that it is possible to be happy all the time. We believe that our happiness is based on our circumstances, what we get and don't get, have and don't have. We credit our happiness to what happens to us. And we're wrong.

Happiness as a feeling is fleeting. In that form, it is really pleasure or enjoyment, a signal that we like what we are currently experiencing, and it will pass pretty quickly. Inevitably, other emotions will show up, taking its place, to share their important messages about what's happening to and around us.

Our "good vibes only" culture also sets us up to fail in the happiness department because it perpetuates the myth that we should avoid any sort of discomfort or unpleasant experience, and it drives us to pursue external sources of that prized feeling. In reality, directly chasing happiness backfires.

Instead, we must take a wider lens when it comes to happiness, considering it more as a sense of satisfaction and peace with our overall life experience. I believe that true happiness comes from within—from getting a handle on your mind, surrounding yourself with good people, doing something meaningful, and being true to yourself. It is the side effect of living life well.

SURPRISING INSIGHTS ABOUT LASTING HAPPINESS

On Friday mornings, I work out with my trainer, Emily. This is a pretty recent and very positive development in my life. With her unwavering support and perfectly timed pushes, she's teaching me, building my strength and my confidence, and helping me reach my goals (Michele Obama arms and 10 push-ups). I find myself (surprisingly) looking forward to the creative tortures she designs for me each time. Today's wrapped up with a grueling round of conditioning: six 45-second intervals of explosive exercises. At the end, with my heart slamming and breath panting, we fist bumped, and I prepared for my short walk home. My heart continued to pound the whole way, and it took a solid 15 minutes or so for my breath to fully return to normal and for my body to achieve homeostasis. But I'm so glad it did.

Homeostasis is defined as a self-regulating process by which an organism maintains a relatively stable internal environment in the face of external changes. In other words, it's our body's ability to return to baseline when things throw it for a loop. It's the reason my heart rate and breathing slowed this morning. Can you imagine what would happen if our bodies weren't designed to do this? If our heart rates didn't settle back down after being elevated by exercise or adrenaline? At this morning's intensity, I'd be dead within the week!

Homeostasis is a good thing... and it's one of the reasons lasting happiness is so hard to find.

IT'S IMPOSSIBLE FOR HAPPINESS TO LAST

Homeostasis isn't just a goal for our physiological systems. It applies to our psychological ones as well. That means that when something happens that makes us happy, say, we get something we really want like a new item or achievement, the high fades pretty quickly. Our brains seek homeostasis, and we return to baseline. This makes happiness elusive. We're not going to get—and keep— happiness indefinitely, contrary to what a lot of people believe is possible.

When you stop and really think about it, this is a brilliant design feature from Mother Nature. If happiness were something we could easily get and keep forever, we'd lose our drive. We'd have no reason to strive for anything again and would basically become big lumps of nothing. Thus, happiness, by nature, is fleeting.

Yet, I do believe lasting happiness is possible. It just requires a complete reengineering of how we think about it.

WHAT IS HAPPINESS?

Through a series of luck and good fortune, I ended up being able to attend TEDxKC. If you're not familiar, this kind of event involves a series of TED-style talks in which dynamic speakers spread big ideas in 18 minutes or less. It was inspiring and expansive. One of my favorite talks was by Arthur Brooks, a professor at Harvard School of Business, prolific author, podcast host, and happiness expert. Dr. Brooks spoke about the keys to lasting happiness, and I could not wait to share his insights.

The first adjustment in our thinking we have to make when it comes to lasting happiness is how we even define what happiness is. Dr. Brooks made the point that happiness is multi-faceted and that it includes so much more than the pursuit of pleasure or the experience of the simple emotion we call "happiness." According to him, there are three components to real happiness: enjoyment, meaning and purpose, and satisfaction.

Without spoiling his entire talk (it's well-worth watching), he highlighted a couple paradoxical points. Besides the one we've already covered—that we are designed to return to baseline so a perpetually elevated state is biologically impossible—he challenged another widely held belief: unhappiness is bad. The cultural myth that we can—and should—be happy at all times is backwards and harmful. It's not possible, for one, and it diminishes the role of pain in happiness.

Wait. Isn't happiness really the *absence* of pain? No. *Pleasure* is the absence of pain, and pleasure is just one tiny slice of the happiness pie. Pleasure is a sense of *I like this* in this moment. It factors into the enjoyment aspect of happiness if you think of enjoyment as pleasure + a recognition and appreciation of the moment and a cognitive appraisal that this is good. Enjoyment alone, however, is not enough for lasting happiness. We get sated and return to baseline. Think of the first yummy bite of ice cream compared to the 100th. You get bored of the flavor and bloated with fullness. Enjoyment decreases over time. More is not better, and the constant chase of pleasure will actually end in pain.

That's why all of the leading thinkers and researchers in the field of happiness, from ancient philosophers to modern scientists, know that lasting happiness includes more than just feeling good in the moment and that pain is unavoidable and, perhaps, even beneficial.

When we consider meaning and purpose, a foundational contributor to our happiness and wellbeing, we must consider that it often arises from pain or hardship or, flatly put, unhappiness. It is often our struggles that illuminate our path toward purpose. Heartbreak and hardship can provide the impetus for our passion and for work that gives us a sense of meaning. And without that preceding pain, we may not find this important component of happiness.

Pain, struggle, and unhappiness are integrally interwoven with satisfaction as well. I can tell you that I decidedly did NOT enjoy struggling through pull-ups this morning with Emily. It was physically hard and uncomfortable. Mentally, it made me aware of my current weakness, and I had to fight the urge to give up (not that she would let me). Yet, I endured that displeasure, that discomfort because I know that on the other side of it lies a sense of satisfaction. I know that I will be happy when I can knock out those push-ups in the not so distant future. That feeling of pride, worth it-ness, and accomplishment contributes to our happiness and wellbeing, but it demands a measure of unhappiness to get there.

If we can take these insights into account—embracing the fleeting nature of happiness and its intricate link to unhappiness—we may be freer, especially in the face of inevitable pain and discomfort, knowing that it is an important and recurring stop on the path to lasting happiness, a prerequisite to meaning and satisfaction. We can challenge ourselves to expand and be willing to embrace this dark side knowing that pain and joy are two sides of the same coin. And in doing so, we may just find more happiness overall.

"The key to happiness is not being rich; it's doing something arduous and creating something of value and then being able to reflect on the fruits of your labor."

—ARTHUR C. BROOKS

BALANCING STRIVING FOR THE FUTURE WITH BEING IN THE PRESENT

My friend, Natalie, lives a different lifestyle than most people I know. When we met 16 years ago, she was doing the house in the suburbs, corporate 9-5 thing. Now she spends half the year in Alaska as a chef and deckhand on a private charter boat and the rest of the year traveling.

She bravely embarked on this epic experiment 10 years ago, before I even knew what life design was. While most of our mutual friends thought she was crazy to leave the security of her salary and 401K to pursue adventure, I thought she was courageous... and I envied her. She was willing to take some risks and carve her own path, and 10 years later, she has no regrets.

While I don't see foresee moving to Alaska in my future, she inspired me to question the rules about how to live life.

LIVING SIMPLY

A few years back, Natalie spent the winter in the Philippines, volunteering to do whale shark research. The budget was about $10 a day... for ALL of the volunteers to share. They lived simply, much like the destitute locals, going to the market daily to get food for dinner and forgoing many of the basic comforts that most of us take for granted (like indoor plumbing and hot showers).

I won't lie. I was horrified when she described her living conditions.

Yet, what she said stuck with me. "My days are full. I'm not bored, but there is absolutely no stress. I'm happy."

How could that be?

THE FISHERMAN AND THE CEO

I am reminded of a story I came across a while back. It goes something like this: A rich American, the CEO of a successful company, took a vacation to a beautiful island. He went fishing one day with a local fisherman. As they sat in the small primitive boat casting their lines, the American said, "You know, if you went out a few extra hours every day, you'd catch more fish, and you could sell the extras at the market."

"Why would I want to do that?" the fisherman asked.

"So you could make more money and get a second boat," said the CEO.

"I don't need a second boat," the fisherman replied. "What would I even do with it?"

"But if you had a second boat, you could grow your operation. You could hire someone to work for you, and you'd catch twice as many fish. You could sell more fish in more markets and make more money. Then, you could expand even more, maybe even selling your fish in the U.S. Then you'd really make a lot of money," the CEO explained. "That's what I would do."

"Once you've got a huge business and are making all of that money, what would you do?" asked the fisherman.

"I'd spend my time fishing," the CEO said, the irony lost on him.

STRIVING V. BEING

As someone who is ambitious, I regularly think about what's next. How do I grow Peak Mind? How do we help more people? Should I write a book? (Obviously, yes on that one.) It seems like there's always a striving toward more, different, better, bigger. There's a pursuit, driven by a longing, an inherent dissatisfaction with the present. Yet there is also an energy and a sense of purpose that can accompany striving for—and reaching—goals.

At the same time, I also spend a TON of time thinking about, researching, and trying to figure out this happiness thing. Being present and accepting things as they are, being grateful, and letting go of unnecessary struggle or yearning seem to be key.

Equally important yet seemingly incompatible, I find myself questioning the balance between striving and being. Who has it right? The CEO or the fisherman?

IS STRIVING WORTH THE STRESS?

Life is inherently stressful, and I don't believe that stress is all bad. But, chronic, poorly managed stress is taking a toll on all of us. The leading causes of ill health are tied to stress. It strains our relationships and drains our wellbeing. And a lot of it is self-imposed and absolutely unnecessary.

We put pressure on ourselves to meet unreasonably high standards. We over schedule and over commit out of perceived obligations to ourselves, to others, and to our futures. We buy into consumerism and the promise that our happiness can be bought.

But it's a lie.

The equation for happiness isn't having what you want. It's wanting what you have.

I don't know that I have the answer yet for balancing striving and being. Maybe it's a both/and rather than an either/or. Maybe it's just about being intentional and making sure that our values, not societal pressures or prescriptions, are dictating our decisions. Maybe it's just important that we pause and examine what we're doing and why we're doing it. Are we pummeling down a path that has been laid out for us without question? Are we pursuing the things that truly matter to us? What sacrifices are we making in the name of striving? Do we really need to make those sacrifices? Are we caught up in keeping up with the Joneses? Are our pursuits causing us more stress than is necessary? How might we simplify things in our life? And what might happen if we actually did?

"The greatest wealth is to live content with little."

—PLATO

HOW OPEN-MINDED ARE YOU?

I went to Orlando to speak at the Going Beyond Vision Loss Summit. I was really excited for a number of reasons. This was my first time speaking to a young audience (14-24-year-olds with some degree of blindness), my first time speaking to a visually impaired audience as a member of the community, and my first time debuting a creative new talk that I was hopeful would land well.

I've done a lot of speaking over the years, and I'm used to these being positive experiences for me. Speaking is something I enjoy, and I think my passion generally comes through. Audience feedback has, fortunately, always been positive, which contributes to my enjoyment and confidence. I've also had really collegial, bordering on friendly, working relationships with event planners, so it's an all-around good time in my book. I expected very much the same thing this time around, but this event was different from the get go.

THE SURPRISES BEGIN

I joined the two event planners for brunch the day before and felt an immediate camaraderie that went well beyond professional niceties and common ground. As I asked about the inspiration for the event, I quickly began to realize just how special these two women were. From a business standpoint, they dreamed up something new and innovative and were able to execute it, ending up with more than double their goal in registrations. I was impressed.

I thought I was coming to town to speak at a one-day event, but the Summit was the kickoff for a multi-day, immersive experience for the attendees that involved staying in AirBnbs, touring a college, going to Disney World, and learning how to be independent with vision loss.

I began to feel grateful for this opportunity, which came up simply because I reached out and suggested that I might be a good speaker for their event. I figured the worst thing that could happen was that they said, "No thanks." I was rewarded for taking a chance.

The unanticipated rewards didn't stop there. I instantly hit it off with one of the other speakers, a 30-year-old man who is into gaming despite a significant vision impairment, and his mom, who was there as his "momager" to help him navigate. I abandoned my plans to chill out and explore on my own to have dinner with them, and I am so glad I did. I felt a genuine sense of friendship and connection in such a short amount of time. I was surprised, and my cup felt full.

Heading into the event, I felt like part of a team rather than someone who was dropping in to do my part, mic drop, and walk away. I felt myself shift from viewing this as a good professional opportunity to being so appreciative that this amazing, rich experience had presented itself to me.

THE SUMMIT

I remember what it was like to be a teen. I was insecure and completely unwilling to publicly embrace my vision impairment. I tried to imagine what 14-year-old Ashley needed to hear, and I crafted a talk for her.

I told these young people that their lives are epic adventures, and they are the heroes of their stories. We focused on building courage and recognizing our unique strengths, all couched within a little brain science because I just wouldn't be me without that piece.

I expected to inspire them and push them out of their comfort zones. Maybe I did. By all accounts, the talk was a success. But I think they inspired me more than the other way around.

These brave, open young people navigated new terrain, approached new people, and spoke in front of a packed ballroom... all with some degree of blindness. I know 14-year-old Ashley would have been awed. 42-year-old Ashley certainly was.

It didn't stop there. There was a 13-year-old girl diagnosed with Usher Syndrome, a condition that causes both blindness and deafness, as well as dyslexia, a learning disability that severely impacts one's ability to learn to read, WHO STOOD UP AND READ A SPEECH about the importance of self-advocacy.

Public speaking is THE number one fear. The joke in the anxiety world is that people would rather be in the casket than giving the eulogy. Yet, here was this young one with barely more than a decade of life under her belt not only braving the number one fear, but also reading in front of a crowd despite dyslexia and vision loss just to show the world that she could and that her disabilities are not limitations. Wow.

THE FLIGHT HOME

As I prepared to leave Orlando, feeling energized, connected, inspired, and humbled, I was also tired. I had gotten up a lot earlier than usual to catch my flight, and I was looking forward to sleeping the entire way home. I boarded in group C, so I excitedly snagged the unexpected remaining aisle seat next to a man my father's age wearing a starched cowboy shirt and cowboy hat... and he began talking before the plane was even finished boarding.

Oh, my god. What have I done? I thought. I'm a talker in general, but not on flights. This was a 2.5+ hour flight. Read that as: an eternity. *I don't want to talk,* I internally groaned.

Sure, I could've politely said I was tired or pulled out my kindle app. Instead, riding high from the previous couple of days, I fully leaned in. I learned all about cattle farming and his grandkids. As his wife joined in the conversation, we chatted about how they met, a life-altering accident she was in, and our shared belief that talking to strangers is a good thing. We exchanged contact information, and the flight flew by. I deplaned before they did and found myself waiting at the gate to hug them goodbye.

Weird, right? That was definitely a first for me.

OPENNESS

The event and the flight served as a one-two punch to reinforce how important openness is. Openness is a personality trait or attribute that has to do with how open-minded and willing to embrace new experiences you are. People with a high degree of openness tend to see value in all experience, regardless of whether you'd deem it "good" or "bad." Research has demonstrated many benefits of openness such as higher cultural intelligence and learning acquisition, better relationships, creativity, and psychological wellbeing.

Whereas some personality traits like extraversion and introversion are equally beneficial—I don't believe that one is better than the other; they are different and both have merits—I think openness is more adaptive than being closed off. In a nutshell, being open exposes you to more possibilities for growth, change, and wellbeing (and yes, even happiness). I think we would all benefit from a collective shift toward more openness.

While many people may argue that personality is a relatively stable thing, I see it as highly malleable. Personally, I have found that a lifestyle practice of intentionally seeking out new experiences has resulted in increasing levels of openness, which makes sense to me. The more we practice something, the easier it gets, and the more natural it becomes.

THE UNEXPECTED CHURROS

As I think about openness, I think about churros. Hang in there. I'll connect those dots.

A while ago, I met up with four amazing women, who are also anxiety specialists. Once upon a time, we all worked at the same place before eventually venturing into private practice. We still get together routinely to consult on cases, talk business, offer support, and just celebrate our friendship. The last time we did was a lesson in openness.

Let me set the scene. We met at a sports bar and grill in Johnson County, an affluent suburb of Kansas City. The menu was strictly American food. Think burgers, sandwiches, and fries. I had already eaten, so I was really only interested in dessert.

Somehow the topic of churros and how much I love them came up, which led to one of us mentioning them to the server, who responded with, "Let me see what I can do."

AND THEN SHE CAME BACK WITH A PLATE OF HOT, FRESH CHURROS!

This place did not have an "it's okay to order off menu" vibe, and there was nothing Mexican food on the menu. And yet, I got delicious churros. It wouldn't have happened without openness—for us to ask the server, for her to ask the kitchen. Talk about unexpected... and delightful!

THE LESSON

So what's the moral of the story here? Step outside of your judgments and expectations. Open yourself to unforeseen possibilities and be present enough to catch glimpses of them. You never know when life is going to give you churros.

"Always be open to inspiration. You never know where it may come from. Begin with an open mind, end with an inspired heart."

—SHERI FINK

HAPPINESS IS NOT PERFECTION

You know that classic job interview question, "What's your biggest weakness?" Conventional wisdom says to give an answer that's really a strength masquerading as a weakness. The perfect answer? "I'm a bit of a perfectionist."

But is that really a sneaky way of showcasing your strengths, or is perfectionism actually a weakness?

There's absolutely nothing wrong with wanting to do well or being a high achiever, but as a (mostly recovered) perfectionist myself, I'd argue that crossing into perfectionism territory is not a good thing and that it may actually cause you more harm than you realize.

RECOGNIZING PERFECTIONISM

At its core, perfectionism is driven by anxiety and rigidity. It stems from fear of failure, rejection, or feeling uncomfortable or out of control. It can manifest in a number of different ways.

High Standards for Self or Others

High standards are the quintessential calling card of perfectionism. It sets an impossibly high bar that, even if you manage to reach it, just raises again, staying always a little out of reach. This can show

277

up in the pursuit of straight A's in school or perfect evaluations at work. It can show up as unrealistic expectations about never making a mistake, being overly concerned with always saying or doing the right thing, or simply a driving need to be your best or THE best possible at whatever it is you're doing.

Sometimes these unrealistic expectations take the form of unyielding demands for how things should be. Rather than being driven to be the best, it's a rigid adherence to the ideas you have in mind. *This is how it should be. This is what should happen. This is how things should be done... and others should willingly follow along.* These shoulds hold reality hostage leaving you feeling angry or upset or out of control when your expectations are not met.

Just Right Perfectionism

Just right perfectionism is another flavor in which high levels of distress arise when things aren't "right." This may mean when things don't look right (e.g., being really bothered by a crooked frame on the wall) or feel right (e.g., like when you have to do something over again until it feels just right). The issue is that things seldom stay "just right" forever, and you're left being agitated when they aren't.

Social Perfectionism

Perfectionism can show up socially, urging you to present yourself in a particular way, trying to match up to some idealized version of what you think others want or expect. You carefully craft a public persona, perhaps through your appearance (not a hair out of place), your online profiles, or the way you interact with others personally or professionally. Social perfectionism can keep you from being real, authentic, or honest for fear of being shunned, judged, or rejected or for fear of being the cause of others' distress.

Indecisiveness

Another surprising way that perfectionism comes out is indecisiveness. People who struggle to make decisions are typically anxious about making the wrong decision or not making the best decision possible.

THE PROMISES OF PERFECTIONISM

Underneath the fear that drives perfectionism is a promise. Like the pot of gold at the end of a rainbow, perfectionism promises that it is the path to some coveted treasure like success, comfort, control, or confidence, and that, ultimately, you will be happy when you reach it.

If you get good enough grades, you'll get into a good college. Keep up the perfect work, and you'll get a good job. Work hard there so you can get promotions and higher salaries so you can what?

Be happy!

Perfectionism in other areas works the same way. Be the best, and good things are guaranteed to happen. You'll be confident and feel unshakably good about yourself. Be perfect socially, avoid judgment or rejection, gain acceptance, and you'll be happy. If things don't look or feel right, you'll be bothered forever. Fix them, and you'll be comfortable and happy. If things go exactly according to your plan, you'll feel in control and be happy. Check off all the boxes when it comes to your career, your partner, and your life, then you'll be happy.

Happiness is the grand prize at the end of the perfectionism promise, but does it actually deliver?

THE COSTS OF PERFECTIONISM

You could argue the whole "Shoot for the moon. If you miss, you'll land among the stars" thing, staking that aiming for perfection and falling short will pay off. I'd argue against it, though. Perfectionism comes with some costs.

Unhappiness

Does the pursuit of perfection really make you happy? Think about your actual experience here, not some imagined future. Do you enjoy the process of striving for perfect, or do you feel "ick"—stressed, frustrated, anxious, angry, or full of doubt? Sure, that moment of reaching that high bar may be glorious... for a second. But, how long does it actually last? Doesn't the target just move again, and the pressure to perform at that highest level just returns? Whatever happiness, comfort, or control you get vanishes pretty quickly.

Shrinking Acceptability Zone

The more you give into perfectionism, the more it demands... and the range of acceptable outcomes shrinks, making you more rigid and inflexible, which actually diminishes your resilience. If you must get all A's, for example, it won't be long before an A is no longer enough. Now it has to be an A+. Eventually, the target will be a 100%. Anything less is unacceptable. The acceptability zone went from 10% (an A in a lot of U.S. schools is 90% or higher, so 90-100% is good enough), to only one outcome is okay (100%). Similarly, the more you try to control everything that happens, the more you'll be thrown off when things don't go according to plan. And let's be real, when does life ever go according to plan?

Damage to Relationships

Perfectionism takes a toll on relationships in a number of ways. If you're adhering to those expectations you have in mind and forcing them onto others, they're going to feel like you're trying to control them. That can cause tension in relationships, and resentments can grow.

If you're wrapped up in social perfectionism and that's leading to inauthenticity, you're actually going to feel less connected. While others may accept you, there will be a nagging doubt in the back of your mind that whispers, *But if they knew the real you, they wouldn't.* Vulnerable authenticity is the way to true connection.

Perhaps the one relationship that takes the biggest hit when it comes to perfectionism is the one you have with yourself. If that Inner Critic is loud, constantly pointing out the ways in which you fall short and pushing you to do better, be better, it's kind of hard to actually feel good about yourself.

Procrastination

Procrastination is a complex habit, but it is often intricately linked to perfectionism. It's natural to want to avoid things that are hard or uncomfortable. If you're on the perfection path, then it's quite likely that tasks take a lot of effort and energy (more than they actually need). When you're faced with those demands, you may find yourself putting off getting started. The pressure to produce at a really high level can also be paralyzing. If you're afraid that it won't be good enough or are unsure about how to move forward (e.g., because it's hard to make a decision), you may find yourself stuck, at least until the deadline is looming large enough to push you forward.

Avoidance and Inaction

Sometimes it goes beyond procrastination to full on avoidance or inaction preventing you from taking a step forward or doing something that feels risky. In that case, perfectionism is actually limiting your success, not enhancing it. It's kind of twisted like that.

BREAKING FREE FROM PERFECTIONISM

There are times when striving for perfection may absolutely be worthwhile, realistic, and important. Often, however, our minds oversell the importance of the task, demanding more than is actually necessary. Perfection should be the exception, not the rule. Learning to lower your standards and accept that good enough is good enough is the key to breaking free from perfectionism.

First, understand that lowering your standards is not the same as failure or even mediocrity. You can do good work, even great work, without succumbing to the drive for perfection. Being able to set perfectionism aside when it does not serve you is the goal here.

Ask yourself:

* Is perfection realistic or even possible in this particular case?

* Is it worth the extra time and energy it will take to pursue perfection?

* Will it actually make a meaningful difference if you/it is perfect or not? Are you 100% sure that it will?

* Are others who have the outcome you're shooting for also perfect?

If you truthfully answer these questions, you'll most likely have to acknowledge that perfection doesn't actually matter that much in this specific case. So, challenge yourself to do less. Shoot for good enough.

If perfectionism is a habit for you, chances are you'll struggle to accept good enough. You'll need to work a little more intentionally on breaking free from perfectionism. To do this, you'll need to practice good enough... a lot. Keep in mind that the more you do it, the easier it will get. Eventually, it will feel natural. When it does, *you'll* be in charge, not perfectionism, which means you'll be able to set your effort level based on what serves you in that moment. In other words, you'll still be able to aim high when you need to but will more easily be able to let it go and settle for good enough when that serves you better, freeing up your time and energy for the things that truly matter.

There are a ton of ways to practice good enough on purpose. Some to consider include:

* Leaving a typo in an email or text.

* Saying something without scripting it out first.

* Messing up your hair or dressing a little slouchier than normal.

* Posting an unfiltered or not quite so flattering picture.

* Leaving something "wrong" (e.g., make the bed "wrong," leave dishes in the sink, let a picture be crooked)—challenge yourself to see how long you can go without fixing it.

* Making a snap decision without overthinking it.

* Letting someone else be in charge of planning and practicing going with the flow.

- Looking for opportunities to fail. (I love the story of how Sara Blakely, founder of Spanx, a wildly successful company, shared that her dad used to ask her everyday as a child, "How did you fail today?" If she didn't have an answer, he'd be disappointed. This approach all but guarantees that fear of failure will never be an obstacle.)

I'm sure another hour of tweaking would make this piece more polished, better in some way. BUT I'm going to call it good enough and go enjoy lunch with some friends.

"Don't let the perfect be the enemy of the good."

—VOLTAIRE

IT'S ALL ABOUT THE LITTLE THINGS

My little brother is a beast. He is incredibly in shape, and it's not genetic luck. He's put in the years of hard work to figure out his optimal nutrition, and he puts in serious time at the gym. He's experimented enough that he knows what to eat and how to work out to increase strength or cut weight to show off muscle definition or bulk up, whatever. He's a whiz at sculpting his physique.

I, on the other hand, try to be active but, like so many, struggle to be disciplined. In my head, I believe wholeheartedly that strength training is critical for health and wellbeing. My actions, however, speak the truth—that I'd rather do anything but. Besides, I get overwhelmed sifting through all of the advice out there to figure out what I actually should be doing to get the results I want. Should I do tons of reps with little weights? Fewer reps with heavy weights? Functional training? Isometrics? Kettlebells? I don't even know where to start!

My brother is also one of the most inspiring people in my circle. I always leave our conversations feeling ready to take on the world and to be a better version of myself. For these reasons, I was really looking forward to asking his advice when we were together in Fort Worth a couple weeks ago for our nephew's graduation.

"Hey, kiddo. I want to get buff fast. What should I do?"

His answer blew my mind a bit.

SURPRISE WISDOM

I was looking for a plan, detailed instructions on what to eat and how to exercise. Instead, what I got was actually beyond useful.

"Honestly, Ash, the best advice I can give you is to do whatever you can do consistently."

His advice was like a lightbulb going off. Duh! Of course, consistency is the highest priority. I could have the optimal fitness plan, but if I can't (or won't) follow it, for whatever reason, I'm not going to get results. It was freeing to cut through all of the noise and feel good about focusing on one top priority: just be consistent. Walk, yoga, run, dance, regret catching the occasional HIIT class. All of these will move me toward my goal. That conversation helped me realize that I was letting the pursuit of the best get in the way of progress.

It got me thinking about how many other places and in how many other ways this mindset might apply. Where do we tend to seek out the best, the perfect, the right, the big payoff, or the grand gesture to our detriment? Where does focusing on big moves lead us to be ineffective or, worse, take no action at all?

THE DANISH SECRET TO HAPPINESS

Right around this same time, I stumbled across the Danish concept of hygge (pronounced "hoo-ga"). Denmark consistently ranks as one of the happiest nations on Earth despite having long, dark winters. I'd venture to say that a culture based on hygge is one of the main reasons.

Hygge is cozy, warm, connected moments. It's candlelight instead of harsh overheads. It's snuggling up with a warm blanket in a welcoming nook to read or playing board games with your best buds. It's comfort food and comfortable silence, laughter and intimacy. It's coffee shops with close friends over bars with strangers. And it's a priority built into every day.

In the U.S., I think we often look toward big, noticeable outside things to bring us happiness—shopping, vacations, dream dates and jobs, promotions or achievements—and we underestimate the cumulative effect that little moments of cozy pleasure may have on us.

What if we took that same "whatever you can do consistently" mentality and applied it here? What if we made efforts to design our daily experience—our activities and our environments—to promote hygge? I can't help but think that would pay dividends in terms of happiness.

THE FOUNDATION OF STRONG CLOSE RELATIONSHIPS

Similarly, frequent small things trump grand gestures when it comes to relationships. Psychologists Drs. John and Julie Gottman are the world's leading experts in couple relationships, with about 40 years of research under their belts. They can predict with near-perfect precision which couples will stay together happily and which will not simply by observing them talk for a few minutes. Based on all of their research and knowledge, the Gottmans advocate for small things often.

It's the little moments that build—or break—your relationships. A grand gesture of rom-com proportions might make for a good story, but it won't erase the damage of speaking unkind words or ignoring your partner's bids for attention on a daily basis. When it comes to healthy, happy relationships, it's the small things, repeated frequently—a habit of relationship-boosting interactions, if you will—that matters most.

LIFE DESIGN AND POSITIVE HABITS

I'm a big proponent of life design—a process for experimenting your way toward a life aligned to you. A key aspect of life design is iteration—designing an experiment, testing it out, then tweaking. It hinges on a bias toward action. Take the step, have the experience, let that experience be your guide, then take another step. Let's carry this attitude and my little brother's wisdom forward to every domain of life.

* Consistency matters most if you're looking to change habits.

* Small changes are easier to maintain than big ones.

* Small things, repeated often, pay off with big results.

Can you imagine what life might feel like if we focused on doing the little things that matter consistently?

"Success is the product of daily habits—not once-in-a-lifetime transformations."

—JAMES CLEAR

IF YOU WANT TO BE HAPPY, EXPECT LESS

A s a teenager, I was stoked to watch *An American Werewolf in Paris*. I just knew it was going to be edgy and scary—a cinematic masterpiece! What it was, however, was a giant let down. It was a terrible movie.

Fast forward a couple years, and said movie was on TV. I agreed to watch it with some friends, despite knowing how much it sucked. Imagine my surprise when the credits rolled, and I realized that I didn't hate it. In fact, I had rather enjoyed it the second go round.

Same movie, polar opposite reactions to it. What accounted for the difference? That experience was one of the first that really hit home to me the power of expectations.

THE POWER OF EXPECTATIONS

Expectations are internally constructed rules and demands for the future—our whats and hows about upcoming situations, events, and even people.

Notice the language: internally constructed. Our brains create expectations, these powerfully adhered to artifacts of imagination; they are not tangible facets of reality or valid parts of our External

World. Sure, some expectations are mutually agreed upon and accepted by a large number of society. (I expect people to wear pants in public, and I venture that you hold the same expectation.) Others, however, are more unique to us as individual expectors, based on our histories, personalities, thought patterns, and wants. Unmet expectations, as in my silly movie example, are frequently the source of angst. Think of your most saddening, maddening, or frightening experiences recently. Think of the times when you felt anything but happy. Were unmet expectations, on your part or someone else's, at the core of the issue?

EXPECT LESS

A pessimist dressed in a realist's clothing may say, "Expect less to avoid disappointment." Set that bar low. Things either turn out just the way you expected, or you're pleasantly surprised.

I agree with "expect less," though in a different way. Expect less. As in expect less frequently. Set fewer expectations period. Don't set the bar lower, but rather, don't set the bar at all. It is the bar itself, not its location, that is the problem. More precisely, it's the mismatch of the bar and reality that robs us of happiness. So much of what happens around us and to us is, at least in part, out of our direct control. Yet, we strive to control it anyway. These efforts give us the illusion of control but really just take time and energy, keeping us from being fully authentic in the moment. If the mismatch of expectations and reality is what fuels discontent, and we can't actually control (at least some aspects of) reality, why not focus on expectations? Those ARE within our sphere of control. Since we can't always predict or predestine events, trying to match expectations to the unknown future is a gamble, and I, for one, am not willing to bet my happiness like that. If we let go of expectations (or don't make them in the first place) then we are free to experience things as they happen. While not every moment will be an enjoyable one that we'd like to have continue or repeat, our overall happiness level is less impacted.

CHALLENGE: Practice embracing some uncertainty. Try to enter into some experiences without imagining or planning how it's going to go. Try to catch and erase your expectations about someone else before you interact. Let go of those shoulds.

EXPECTATIONS AND RELATIONSHIPS

The role of expectations within the context of relationships is particularly interesting to consider. How many times have you found yourself saying or thinking, "I'm mad because I thought you were going to do XYZ?" What you're really saying is that you're angry because your expectations and reality did not match. Maybe you've been on the other side and found yourself apologizing for someone's disappointment in you… for something you did not agree to or weren't even aware was an issue? How was I supposed to know that you expected me to notice that you were quiet because you had a rough day at work? I was too busy setting my own expectations about how this evening was going to go.

Can you imagine what it might feel like for you and your loved ones if we all let go of expectations and worked toward fully accepting each other and ourselves for who and what we actually are?

CHALLENGE: The next time you find yourself angry with someone, check yourself. Did they really do anything wrong, or did they just not meet your expectations? And the next time you find yourself apologizing, ask yourself the same thing.

WRAPPING IT UP

To a certain extent, I believe that we all set expectations. It's one of those shortcuts that allow our brains to process so much information so quickly and to keep us safe. If I expect that running across the interstate may result in me getting hit by a car, I may take precautions. So often though, we make so many internal demands that we essentially hold the future hostage. Meet our demands or else!

The saying "It is what it is" sounds like a vague platitude, but it's more profound than you may realize. It is the essence of letting go of expectations, of meeting each moment as it comes, making room for and accepting the ups and downs of life. It is at the core of being mindful and a key for facilitating your own happiness. I expect that you'll agree.

"With mindfulness, loving kindness, and self-compassion, we can begin to let go of our expectations about how life and those we love should be."

—SHARON SALZBERG

SOCIAL CONNECTION: A KEY TO HAPPINESS

Social connection—the authentic joining, however brief, of my humanness to yours—is a key contributing factor to happiness. The truth is, these days, we are constantly connected... to the Internet and to others' carefully crafted social personas. In this digital age, we have more "connections" than we've ever had: tons of Facebook friends, oodles of Instagram followers, the Twitterverse (excuse me, X-land), all proffering bits of validation in the forms of likes and shares. We text and email constantly, yet half of us are lonely.

We have an innate psychological *NEED* to feel a sense of belonging and closeness with others, yet the average American adult has fewer close friends now than a generation ago. Perhaps that's because we move farther away and more frequently. Maybe we're "too busy" with other demands and don't have the time or energy to prioritize socializing. Or maybe we don't know how to genuinely connect anymore; we're scared and out of practice, and a pandemic certainly didn't help.

Regardless of the reason, loneliness is an epidemic.

Loneliness is something I've struggled with over the years. "I need more friends and better eyes" was, sadly, a frequent sentiment in my junior high journal entries. As a socially anxious teen, I desperately wished I could be friendly and outgoing, but I was so worried about being negatively judged that I censored myself. I had friends but lacked self-confidence, and lacking confidence leads to wearing metaphorical masks and putting up walls that separate us from others.

No more masks and no more walls. Over the past several years, I've adopted some practices that have made a tremendous difference in my overall happiness level and quality of life (e.g., having new experiences regularly, embracing vulnerability, intentionally building new beliefs through deliberate actions, mindfulness). But seeking out connections—and, more importantly the mindset shift that drives that quest—seems to have had a truly profound impact.

THE MINDSET SHIFT

The importance of actively pursuing social connection crystalized for me a few autumns ago after an evening of unlikely interactions. I went to Irish Fest on my own to join a meetup group that essentially ended up with me as the fifth wheel on a double date. Fortunately, at that point in my life, I had a pretty high tolerance for awkward, so I decided to embrace the situation and try to get to know those people. After parting ways, I took the streetcar home. Energized from the evening, I found myself playing tour guide to a mom and daughter visiting from out of state, then deep in conversation with a man from a very different walk of life. Once home, I reflected on how unexpectedly happy I felt and drew some essential conclusions.

I realized that every single person whose path I cross is a potential connection. I don't know if the person next to me is my future best friend, the love of my life, my next business partner, or just a drop of connection to remind me that I am not alone, that I am a part of humanity. That night illustrated the power of being open to connecting with others, even for fleeting moments.

THE UBER ATTITUDE ADJUSTMENT

Because Uber is my primary mode of transportation, I am constantly in close quarters with strangers, faced with the options of conversing or sitting in silence (realistically, burying myself in a tiny screen). My tendency to opt for the former is continually reinforced. I've had drivers who unexpectedly inspire me, introduce me to new genres of music, technology, and restaurants, make me laugh, and broaden my horizons culturally and philosophically.

One driver in particular left a lasting impression a few years ago. Obinna, a young African man, dramatically improved my day and changed my outlook. The conversation started like any generic small talk: "The weather is beautiful today!" he said.

"I know! I'd much rather be outside enjoying it than going to the office, especially because I don't usually work on Fridays."

A joke about trading places. A question about why I was working on a different day than usual.

"Well, I just got back from Iceland, so I am making up some missed time."

"ARE YOU KIDDING ME!? You just got back from Iceland and you're complaining!?!?" said my driver, smiling, and almost shouting at me.

Wait, what? I thought. I expected a big reaction to Iceland. That's been pretty standard. But he was chastising me about complaining?

Wait. I AM complaining. What the heck?

He continued, "You work so you can be ballin' and go on awesome trips! Be grateful that you get to do that!"

You know, Mr. Uber, you're right! My perspective shifted immediately. *I have patients today. My work has meaning and seeing them allows me to live this lifestyle that I am cultivating and enjoying, and I AM grateful!*

I felt my mood lift, dread replaced with excitement. This young man, this complete stranger from a different continent, changed my day in a way that had ripple effects.

Not everyone with whom I interact has a noticeable positive impact on me, but many do. Rarely, though, have I regretted talking to someone. Usually, the worst case is a neutral experience. Nothing gained, but nothing lost. Regardless of the exchange, though, it, frankly, feels better to be friendly.

WHAT GETS IN THE WAY OF CONNECTING?

In a word: JUDGMENT. Fear of and of others.

Fear of Judgment

Humans are inherently social creatures, and the threat of being ostracized or shunned by the herd triggers fear or anxiety. Therefore, we worry about being judged or rejected by others.

* *He'll think I'm dumb.*

* *She'll reject me if she knows the real me.*

* *I must be the only one who XYZ.*

- *If I share my real opinion, they won't like me anymore.*

- *What if I embarrass myself?*

We are hardwired to escape or avoid anxiety-provoking situations. In this case, that may mean avoiding putting ourselves out there or risking potential rejection. Have you ever held back or censored yourself because you were concerned about what someone else would think about you? Be honest. I know I have.

Judgment of Others

We pre-judge others on the basis of exterior appearances and our own beliefs, and those judgments put up barriers to connecting. Our expectations about others influence how, or even whether, we interact with them.

Nowadays, I find myself embracing strangers… sometimes to the chagrin of those around me. On a trip a few years ago, my friend Michael messaged to virtually introduce me to his friend, who was traveling in the same city. Yay! A friend of my friend has to be cool, right? I immediately followed up with her to set up a time to get together. My travel partner, one of my dearest friends, however, had a completely different reaction when I told her we were meeting for brunch. "What? What if she's weird?" We had a moment of tension as the difference in our underlying mindsets about new people became obvious. (Side note: brunch was quite enjoyable.)

HOW TO MAKE IT HAPPEN

I realize that being friendly or outgoing or open or authentic or whatever word you want to call it is sometimes easier said than done. The good news, though, is that it CAN be done! Here are some key points to keep in mind.

If the fear of being judged holds you back, ask yourself these key questions:

- You can't control what other people think. Why bother?

- What's the worst thing that can happen? You let someone see the real you and they reject you? That sucks, sure, but it won't kill you. Wait, before you move on, consider what's the *best* thing that could happen? You put yourself out there and others accept and value you? What would that experience do for you? Confidence up, insecurity down. Sounds good to me!

- What are five other things they could think (could've thought) in that moment?

Know that it gets easier with practice. That's a concept called graduated exposure—baby steps of putting yourself out there and testing out how others respond.

If your own judgments and expectations get in the way, step out of your own judgments and try people on, so to speak. Did they match your expectations and assumptions?

Make a qualitative shift in how you approach interactions by having the goal of connecting rather than alternative goals like changing the other person, being right, getting something out of it, or protecting yourself from possible threat. For example, I had a super engaging and respectful conversation with a Flat Earther because I chose to be open to trying to understand his perspective rather than trying to prove him wrong or writing him off all together. While we don't share fundamental philosophies, I still got a boost of happiness from that connection. Finding commonalities, especially with people who don't necessarily look or act like you, can restore your faith in humanity and help you feel like you're a part of something bigger than just you.

I challenge you to embrace the mindset that everyone is a potentially worthwhile connection. Doing so has been transformational! It has exponentially increased my openness to interacting with others. It has translated into more frequent conversations with a much wider variety of people and helped to reduce feelings of loneliness, even when key players in my life are far away or haven't entered yet.

The other unexpected outcomes? I have gotten increasingly comfortable being vulnerable, which allows for more authentic connections as well as more self-confidence and acceptance. I am also generally more compassionate and find myself getting less annoyed with others. All in all, I'm just happier.

"I define connection as the energy that exists between people when they feel seen, heard, and valued; when they can give and receive without judgment; and when they derive sustenance and strength from the relationship."

—BRENE BROWN

GIVING OPPORTUNITIES FOR GRATITUDE

A t the end of September, I spoke at an HR event where I met some incredible people. One in particular made a big impact.

Nora is a professional speaker from Denver and the only other person I know who takes new experiences as seriously as I do. (I've made it a point to have at least one a week, every week, since January 2017.) We met by Zoom before the event and then had dinner while she was in town. She was so open about the speaking industry (one I've dabbled in but only recently pushed fully into), imbuing mentorship, wisdom, and advice. I was so grateful for that time together.

Somehow, between our dinner and Nora's lunch with another new-to-the-industry woman named Barb (who, turns out, is practically my neighbor), a plan was hatched for Barb and me to go to Denver for a weekend to learn more about the biz.

Two weeks ago, Barb and I headed to the airport to catch a super early flight for what turned out to be an absolutely incredible experience. Nora had prepared a detailed itinerary and roped eight other phenomenal professional speakers in to impart their knowledge as well.

I'll admit, there was a quiet skepticism in my mind. *Why is she doing this? This is a lot of time and energy to give to two people she barely knows. This is a great opportunity for me, but what is she getting out of it?*

Now, I was raised with Southern manners, and I know better than to look a gift horse in the mouth. Still, it took a bit for it to fully sink in that Nora's motives were truly just a paying it forward kind of thing. She shared her belief that it's important for women to mentor other women and that pouring into others, especially when they are receptive to it and worth it (meaning they're going to utilize the gift being given), is valuable in and of itself.

I was overwhelmed with gratitude. That someone would see potential in me and want to nurture it like that. That someone would be willing to dedicate their time, energy, and effort in such a real and concentrated way. That someone would welcome me into their tribe, with open arms and full support, after knowing me such a short time. That strangers, these other women who had never met me, would also be willing to show up and share the way they did, with no expectation of anything in return.

Wow. I am humbled.

More than once during that weekend and many times since, I've questioned how I got so lucky.

GIVING GRATITUDE OPPORTUNITIES TO OTHERS

Being on the receiving end of such generosity got me thinking. There are really good people all around us. We're so bombarded with gloom and doom and transactional interactions—people trying to sell us or get from us—that it's easy to lose sight of that. There are truly giving people out there, willing to pour into others, and we're all better off for it.

I realized that I am not only grateful for the Denver weekend itself, but also for the opportunity to *be that grateful*. Feeling blessed is a great way to feel.

I think about gratitude a lot. It's a practice that is consistently linked to happiness and wellbeing. But I had never really thought about approaching gratitude from the angle of giving opportunities for it to others, but it's an idea that's percolating.

I want to be clear that I don't mean creating opportunities for others to express gratitude or appreciation to you. It's not about you or what you can get out of it. It's about bestowing that blessed feeling onto someone else.

I'm envisioning more of a pay-it-forward-meets-acts-of-kindness kind of thing where the side effect is that the receiver feels a sense of gratitude. Wouldn't that be wonderful?

I wonder what would happen if more people made an effort to do just that. What if we intentionally poured into others with no expectation in return? What if we focused on building them up, cheering them on, guiding and supporting them? What if we strived to make others feel worthy and grateful?

"I am the recipient of many benefits that I do not deserve and did not earn. Someone else paid for them. I am grateful! How do I show my gratitude? By daily pouring into others and passing on to them the things that will allow them to run far and achieve beyond what I have done."

—JOHN C. MAXWELL

BE LIKE GERDA: FINDING THE BRIGHT SPOTS IN THE DARKEST TIMES

You know those conversations that just stick with you? The ones that don't necessarily seem significant at the time but then worm their way into your memory, take root, and blossom into something that fundamentally shifts your worldview?

Have you ever had that experience secondhand? When you weren't even a part of the original conversation, you just heard the recap? I have, and I want to share that with you.

GERDA'S STORY

A few years ago, back before Peak Mind was even a consideration and April had just gotten into podcasting, she and I were catching up on the phone. She told me about a recent guest she had just interviewed, a woman who survived the Holocaust. April told me that in their conversation, the woman (who I now know is named Gerda Weissman Klein) remarked to her that no one ever talks about the good parts of the Holocaust.

EXCUSE ME?! The *good* parts of the Holocaust? There were *GOOD* parts of the greatest human atrocity of modern times?

Gerda told April about the compassion and support and friendship and sacrifice amongst the Jews in the concentration camps.

I can't even begin to imagine the hardships and suffering that survivors had to endure, and I was blown away that one would highlight the bright spots. Honestly, I was blown away that there even were bright spots. That fact speaks to some of the strengths of the human spirit.

It also put into perspective for me that, no matter how bad things seem, there has to be a bright spot, some positive aspect, some tiny bit of good. It may take a lot of effort to find it, but it's there.

FINDING THE BRIGHT SPOTS

In my clinical practice, I often teach both kids and adults about our brain's natural negativity bias, the importance of finding a "but at least" in every crummy situation, and the power of gratitude. I am often, however, met with a version of "But this sucks! There's nothing good about it."

That's when I share my secondhand conversation with Gerda. If she can find something to be grateful for during the Holocaust, I'm pretty sure we can find something here.

Finding a bright spot, something to appreciate or be grateful for, doesn't negate the pain, the suffering, the hardship, or the adversity you are facing. Those things are real, and they're there. They're hard to ignore, and they tend to demand and hold our attention.

Practicing gratitude—the act of finding and focusing on those bright spots—helps us have a more balanced view of our experience. It helps us to be strong and resilient. It gives us a lifeline to cling to when it feels like we're drowning.

Don't shortchange this practice, though, by quickly naming things you *should* appreciate. Seek out the unique bright spots for that day, and when you find one, *savor it*. Really focus on it, tap into that sense of gratitude, and hold on to it for just a little while. (10-12 seconds to be exact. That's about how long it takes positive stuff to get encoded in our memories, in contrast to the negative stuff that gets socked away pretty much instantaneously.)

And as you work to find your bright spots on even the darkest days, please don't let gratitude become a sneaky way to shame yourself. (*You've got a roof over your head and food to eat. You should be grateful. Why are you struggling?* or *There's always a bright spot. Why can't you find it? What's wrong with you?* Commence self-criticism spiral.) In those moments, perhaps the bright spot is simply that you tried. Amidst everything else going on, you tried, and that speaks to your strength.

Whether your circumstances make it easy or difficult, I implore you to find the bright spots each and every day.

Be grateful. Be strong. Be like Gerda.

"I pray you never stand at any crossroads in your own lives, but if you do, if the darkness seems so total, if you think there is no way out, remember, never ever give up. The darker the night, the brighter the dawn, and when it gets really, really dark, this is when one sees the true brilliance of the stars."

—GERDA WEISSMAN KLEIN

STOP CHOOSING TO SUFFER AND TAKE CHARGE OF YOUR HAPPINESS

"Look around at what you have with appreciation. Be happy with it, and if you aren't, reach a little higher," he said as we sat around the fire, having a surprisingly deep conversation.

Let me rewind.

THE ALASKANS

About five years ago, I was fresh out of a breakup and a few months into what I was terming my Blind Quest for Happiness. I went to Alaska to spend some time with Natalie.

She decided to take me to Petersville, where she had spent the previous winter. Petersville is a tiny little legitimately off-the-grid community. They generate their own power. If they need it, they do it or make it. They hunt moose from their front doors and park their cars for the entire winter, relying on snow machines to get around instead. They are survivors, modern-day frontiersmen (and women).

We planned to just stop in for lunch with Bruce and Demi, but they insisted we stay the night. They opened their home, and their tight-knit little community embraced us.

These Alaskans are the hardiest and heartiest people I've ever met.

One of them, Ernie, reminded me of my dad, and I felt an instant kinship with him. Which brings me back to the fire. As the light waned and we were hanging outside, chatting and sharing a meal with the Petersville people, Ernie and I talked about living in Alaska, relationships, and happiness. That's when he shared his simple, yet profound, wisdom.

In the years since, I've found myself drawing on psychological science to help my patients, friends, and (especially) myself get unstuck, combat negativity, and be happier. I'm leaning on science and theory to do what Ernie knew intuitively: Change your outsides, change your insides, or suffer.

PSYCHOLOGICAL LIMBO LAND

I call it psychological limbo land. That spot where you're not satisfied with your circumstances, but you're not doing anything about it. You're just complaining, venting, and, ultimately, being miserable.

You want a new job, but you're not looking for one. You want to make friends, but you're not putting yourself out there. You want more energy, but you're not going to bed earlier. You want financial security, but you're not saving anything. You want... but you're not...

What it really boils down to is three choices—and yes, they are choices that you are responsible for making:

1. Change your circumstances.

2. Change your attitude.

3. Suffer.

CHANGE YOUR CIRCUMSTANCES

Make a decision or take action to change something in your environment, your day-to-day experience, or your life circumstances. In other words, change your outsides.

Before you start to tell me all the reasons why you can't, I need you to pause and consider. Is it that you *can't*, or is it that you are *unwilling to pay the price*?

Yes, there are some limitations that our circumstances place on us. I am not in the business of denying reality here. I've just seen too many people tell me they can't make a desired change when that's just not factually accurate.

You can't leave your job? Really? Or can you absolutely leave your job IF you are willing to pay the price of uncertainty or financial cutbacks or the discomfort that comes from others' perceived judgment or disappointment?

You can't meet new people? Is that the truth, or are you just unwilling to endure the discomfort that comes from trying, stepping out of your comfort zone, or risking rejection and disappointment?

You absolutely CAN make hard decisions IF you are WILLING to pay the price.

If you're not, that's okay. It absolutely is. I implore you to be precise with your language, though. *I can't* robs you of power, leaving you blameless but also a victim. *I'm unwilling* might force you to be honest with yourself about the choices you are making, which can be painful, but also empowering.

CHANGE YOUR ATTITUDE

There are times when you are unwilling to pay the price or truly cannot make the desired change. It's not a willingness issue. It's a real constraint out of your control or choosing. You still have choice here, though. You can change your insides.

I see so many people who want to feel in control yet readily give it up. They want to control things they can't—others, outcomes, the future—but refuse, intentionally or simply because they don't know it's an option, to control the things they can, things like attention and attitude.

For example, let's say you want to lose weight but are unwilling to learn how to eat for your body's needs and to change sedentary habits. Or perhaps your unwanted weight is the result of hormones or genetics or something that you can't really control or change. Fine. That doesn't mean you have to resign yourself to psychological limbo land, hating your body. You can work on acceptance.

In psychology, acceptance means taking things as they actually are. It's recognizing without amplifying. (The whole just because life gives you a cactus doesn't mean you have to sit on it thing. *I have a cactus. Period.* = acceptance. *I have a cactus. I don't want this cactus. It's ugly and prickly. I didn't ask for it. This sucks.* = sitting on said cactus, causing more pain. Pain + non-acceptance = suffering. The choice is yours.)

Acceptance doesn't mean approving of or liking. It just means that you're not struggling against it any more. You're saying, "It is what it is," and being indifferent, unaffected by it. If you can't or won't change your circumstances, then accept things as they are... and take it a step further by adjusting your attitude.

If you've decided that you absolutely are unwilling to quit your job, cool. You can choose to go to work each day with a grumbly grinchy attitude, letting your built-in negativity bias run unchecked. You can complain about everything that is unfair or unpleasant.

OR

You can adjust your attitude and make the best of it. You can actually force your attention to focus on the parts of your job that don't suck. You can practice gratitude. You can try to learn something new. You can try to connect your work with a bigger meaning. (Is it to provide for your family? Be able to have luxuries in life? Take care of customers?) You can simply choose to put a smile on your face (which can impact your mood, according to research).

The bottom line is you do have choice and control here, just maybe not over what you want.

SUFFER

Suffering is a choice, too. Let that sink in.

We often choose, albeit unknowingly, to suffer. When we hang out in psychological limbo land, that's really all we're doing.

There's a Buddhist teaching that holds that pain is inevitable. Suffering is optional.

Pain *is* inevitable. It's going to happen. Physical pain. Emotional pain. It's a part of life. What we do with that pain, however, is what leads to suffering. Getting stuck in psychological limbo land, refusing to take action, refusing to accept or embrace reality, giving up control of the things over which we actually have it, yearning for something that doesn't exist or isn't possible. That's the path to suffering. It's ours to take. I just wish more people wouldn't.

I know it's hard not to. Believe me. I've had the luxury of decades of psychological training and experience, of walking on healing journeys with thousands of people, and of figuring out my own trudge out of psychological limbo land and learning to accept vision loss. I spent way more time in (unknowingly) self-imposed suffering than I care to admit. I know how hard it can be.

Yet, I also know that we make it harder on ourselves than it has to be by denying reality and wallowing. We want different choices. We want it to be easy, pain-free, fair. We want the rules to be different, to play a different game than the one we're in. But those aren't our choices. Change your outsides. Change your insides. Or suffer. Which will it be?

"Look around at what you have with appreciation. Be happy with it, and if you aren't, reach a little higher."

—ERNIE, **the Alaskan**

EPILOGUE

I'm not really an inspirational quote wood wall art kind of person... but I have a homemade one hanging on the wall outside my office. It reads "Adapt & Conquer." It's a personal motto I stole from my younger brother, Joey. He is 10 years my junior, following in my footsteps of vision loss, yet in many ways, I am following in his. He made peace with our genes long before I did and has inspired me in more ways than I can count.

I love his motto. It reminds me that no matter what happens, I can handle it. I can adapt. I can figure it out. I can overcome.

I hope that you know that, too. I hope that you have gleaned some new insight, some new actionable takeaway through these pages. My wish for you is that your mind and your circumstances do not hold you back, that they do not impede your journey any more than they absolutely have to.

Ultimately, it is up to each of us to take responsibility, not necessarily for what happens to us, but for what we do with it. We cannot control everything, but we can always exercise control over something, even if it's just our attitude. We can become savvy about how our minds work and strive to make them work for us. We can navigate our emotions and our relationships with wisdom and skill. We can make the tough choices and do the hard things to carve out a life that we are proud of, one that reflects who we are and who we want to be. And if we do all of these things, happiness is the inevitable outcome.

I dare you to dream big, to do the impossible, to fully embrace your experience, and to live a bold life, one that Future You can look back on many years from now with a deep knowing and satisfaction that you lived yours well.

"Tell me, what is it you plan to do with your one wild and precious life?"

—MARY OLIVER

ACKNOWLEDGMENTS

I am incredibly fortunate to have so many amazing people in my life who contributed to this book in so many ways—by molding me as a professional and as a person, inspiring me, encouraging and supporting me, taking trips with me, having meaningful conversations, reading my writing, giving me much needed advice, and calling me out. I owe you.

April Seifert, this wouldn't have happened without you on so many levels. Teaming up with one of my dearest friends to build a mission-driven business has been such a wild experience. I have learned more from you than I can possibly put into words. You are a badass, and I aspire to be like you in more ways than one.

Andrea, David, and Joey Smith, I know that you are in my corner, always. I lean on each of you in different ways, and I am grateful for you. Mom, I appreciate you for always giving me opportunities, for truly supporting me (which meant letting me pursue the things I wanted without pressure to live up to any expectations yet pushing me when I needed courage that I didn't yet have), and for introducing me to yoga before it was cool. I love you and your shapes on the wall. Pops, thank you for reading every word of my Master's thesis and all of my blogs. Thank you for never shooting down my dreams and, in fact, adding to them. I should've listened to you years ago when you told me to be a motivational speaker. You were right... just don't let it go to your head. Joey, where do I even start, kiddo? Your influence is woven throughout these pages and throughout my psyche. You motivate me like no one else, and I am so proud of you and proud to be your sister. Zach, be in peace.

Jennifer Ceska and Gail Adams, thank you for being such awesome cheerleaders and supportive fans when April and I started

Peak Mind. G, that's certainly not all you've done or all that I am grateful for. I tell people all the time that my grandmother is cooler than theirs.

Natalie Payn, thank you for inspiring me by living your life the way you do and for being my adventure partner. You are one of my favorite people on the planet, Chica.

Thank you to the rest of my Post-it note people and the friends, both in this book and outside of it, who accepted me when I was so scared that no one would and who helped me learn so many important lessons.

To my Anxiety Ladies—Heather Smith, Lindsey Murray, Amy Jacobsen, and Chris Sexton—you have shaped who I am as a psychologist. Thank you for that, for your friendship, and for your enthusiastic support of all my endeavors. Shala Nicely, thank you for all of that and then some.

I am also grateful for the many other psychologists and professionals who taught, supervised, and mentored me over the years. I am an amalgamation of you, and I like the way things turned out.

To all of my patients, thank you for trusting me to be a part of your journey. While I was teaching you, you were teaching me. It has been a privilege and a gift.

To everyone who is or has been a part of the Peak Mind community, I am grateful for you, too. For investing your time and energy in us and in yourself and for giving me a platform to process things through writing.

Finally, a mighty thanks to Lil Barcaski and the team at GWN Publishing/Virtual Creatives for making this project a reality. I literally could not have done it without you.

BIOGRAPHY

D r. Ashley Smith is an award-winning licensed psychologist, professional speaker, author, co-founder of Peak Mind: The Center for Psychological Strength, and self-proclaimed happiness quester. She is an outspoken advocate dedicated to changing the way we approach mental health and wellbeing. Since earning her PhD in 2007, she has become a sought-after specialist in the treatment of anxiety disorders and is involved in public outreach through the Anxiety and Depression Association of America. In addition to direct patient care, she captivates audiences through her speaking and writing. Publications include books, numerous articles, and a blog, and her speaking consistently gets rave reviews from audiences of all sizes.

Dr. Ashley is also open about living—and learning to thrive—with a rare visual impairment. The combination of her professional expertise and personal experiences put her in a unique position to educate and inspire. She is passionate about using psychology and applied neuroscience to help others live bold, happy lives while performing at their peak.

Made in the USA
Columbia, SC
28 September 2024

42793201R00190